Glasgow's
Airports

Abbotsinch – terminal frontage. The terminal building has been extended considerably beyond its original shape. (Allen Mclaughlin)

Abbotsinch – the outside of the original terminal now forms part of the interior. (Allen Mclaughlin)

Glasgow's Airports

Renfrew and Abbotsinch

Keith McCloskey

The
History
Press

In Memory of
Maxwell Forbes Turner
1925–1988
A Fine Scottish Gentleman

Abbotsinch – the original basic frontage of the terminal with extensions, c.1984. (Photograph by Clive Braham)

First published 2009

The History Press
The Mill, Brimscombe Port
Stroud, Gloucestershire, GL5 2QG
www.thehistorypress.co.uk

© Keith McCloskey, 2009

The right of Keith McCloskey to be identified as the Author
of this work has been asserted in accordance with the
Copyrights, Designs and Patents Act 1988.

British Library Cataloguing in Publication Data.
A catalogue record for this book is available from the British Library.

ISBN 978 0 7524 5077 3

Printed in Great Britain

Contents

Foreword

When Keith approached me to help with aspects of his book I was only too pleased to help, especially as it meant foraging in the loft for old notebooks and nostalgic memorabilia. To be asked to write the foreword is indeed an honour.

Like many who'll no doubt browse and buy this fine book, I too was fascinated by aeroplanes from a young age. In my early teens, during the 1950s, I joined the Air Training Corps and flew in de Havilland Chipmunks and venerable Avro Ansons from Prestwick and Edinburgh (Turnhouse). Departing from the latter airport, I well remember a flight to Perth (Scone) sitting astride a coffin in the aisle of an Anson, and doing the 'penguin waddle' whilst wearing a parachute pack for Chipmunk flights. I also enjoyed ATC Camps with their draughty tents and highly enjoyable greasy fried breakfasts. In 1959 I even gravitated to learning to fly gliders with 662 VGS at HMS *Condor*, RNAS Arbroath. I was hooked.

Fence-hanging, with notebook, pencil, cheap binoculars and a Brownie 127 camera, began for me at Renfrew Airport in mid-1956. Who can forget the elegant terminal building with its triumphant, sweeping arch? How sad I was to hear in later years that this graceful piece of modern architecture had been demolished to make way for a supermarket – truly a travesty.

From the fence could be seen British European Airways (BEA) DC3 Dakotas and (Scottish Aviation Ltd overhauled) Royal Canadian Air Force Sabre jet fighters aplenty. Also seen were BEA Herons as they plied to and from the Western Isles. I often mused about landing on the beach at Barra, but didn't actually achieve it until 2008 … and it was a magic experience well worth the wait.

In late 1956 I made my first foray on my bike to nearby HMS *Sanderling*, Royal Naval Air Station Abbotsinch. There, over the next few years, I suffered from agonising, but blissful, writer's cramp as I noted down the details of 602 Squadron 'City of Glasgow' Royal Auxiliary Air Force Vampires and hundreds of redundant airframes such as Sea Hornets, Attackers, Avengers, Fireflies, Sea Furies, Sea Hawks, Skyraiders, Gannets, Sea Venoms and even newly-built jet fighters like the powerful de Havilland Sea Vixen.

On top of that there were the excellent Navy Air Days from 1957 to the last in 1962 before it closed in 1963 to become the new Glasgow Airport. Who can forget the sweetie drops from a Dragon Rapide and the rugby scrums to catch a toffee? Or the look on the toddlers' faces as they watched a man playing a piano whilst underslung from a helicopter, and the gasp as the line snapped and he plummeted to earth. Fortunately, the dummy was unharmed!

Little did I realise that after joining Air Traffic Control in 1962 I would return to Renfrew that year to commence my controller training. From there I went to Airwork Services Ltd at Scone to do my sponsored PPL flying which, of course, included a flight to Renfrew on 7 July 1962 in Cessna 175 G-AROD to attend the last RNAS Abbotsinch Air Day. One just had to do it! The air station closed in 1963 and the new Glasgow Airport opened in 1966. I continued my ATCO career in London until I retired in 2001 as a Watch Manager at London Terminal Control, West Drayton. However, from 1956 to date I've always been interested in, and written about, the Fleet Air Arm.

Renfrew – the new terminal opened in 1954. (Renfrew Library)

The photographs and historical contents of this book span nearly 100 years; back, in fact, to 29 July 1911 when the famous pilot Colonel S.F. Cody flew to Greenock Road racecourse in Paisley, only a mile or so from where you possibly are now – Glasgow International Airport.

Somehow I feel the final chapters about Renfrew Airport and RAF/RNAS Abbotsinch have yet to be written, not to mention Glasgow's airport as it develops into the future. Enjoy this detailed and well-researched book and revel in Keith's tribute to Glasgow's aviation.

Douglas A. Rough
Taplow
Buckinghamshire
23 February 2009

ACKNOWLEDGEMENTS

I would like in particular to mention three people who have given me considerable help with the legwork to produce this book: Jim Fulton, Fred Seggie and Douglas Rough. I am indebted to them for their considerable assistance and suggestions.

I am also indebted for the story of the Renfrew Zero kindly related by Captain Eric 'Winkle' Brown to Douglas Rough – all the more remarkable because the details were provided from memory just prior to 'Winkle' celebrating his ninetieth birthday.

I would also like to thank the following: Fred Aldworth for background to RCAF flights into Renfrew; Kerry Black and the Scotsman Publications for kindly allowing me the use of their Concorde photograph; Mr Blane; Gordon Lyons; Alasdair McLeod for information relating to the crash of Starways DC3 G-AMRB; Bruce Blanche; Tom Boyle for help with BCAL at Glasgow; Brian Burrage (co founder, www.vickersviscount.net); Dugald Cameron who laid all the groundwork for any future research on Glasgow's airports; Peter Clegg (I am particularly indebted to Peter for his kind help and access to his material on John Sword and Midland and Scottish Air Ferries); Antoin Daltun; Jim Davies for allowing me access to the BA archives and museum; Stewart Davidson; Robert Dixon; Paul Emery; Dr Alastair T. Gardiner; Malcolm Fife for early Renfrew details; Guy Halford-MacLeod; Iain Hutchison for a great deal of help on Scottish aviation and pointing me in the right direction for a number of areas; Peter P. Johnson and Svanbjorn Sigurdsson (Icelandic Aviation Museum) with background on Loftleidir/Icelandic air services; Phil Jones and Geoff Slee for details of 1441 Combined Operations Development Flight; Bjorn Larrson; Philip Lo Bao for the very kind access to his detailed knowledge on BEA operations; Colin Lourie for photos and help with background information; Malcolm MacDonald of Stornoway Historical Society; Thomas MacFadyen for information on WGAF Sabres at Renfrew; Iain MacKay; Colin MacKinnon; Rhoda MacLeod of Dumbarton Library; Elaine Mcgillivray of Mitchell Library; John Martindale; Laura Merivirta of Finavia; Alistair Ness for help with photos; Moira Milne; Shani Pitrola of Euronautical; Gordon Spence who runs the Glasgow Airport website; James Towill and Dougie Martindale (Viking Crash Research) for help with the BEA Viking G-AIVE crash; Gerry Traynor for providing 602 Squadron pictures and material as well as a good deal of support; Richard Wainwright (BAA) – once again!!! – for pulling the proverbial rabbit out of the hat on statistics for both Renfrew and Abbotsinch, for which I am indebted; Robin Walker; Dave Wilton and Colin Smith for superb digging on the USAF at Renfrew; Darren Wheeler for information on Vickers flights; Jim Devine; Guy Henderson and his father Alistair for all the Naval digging and provision of photos; Phillip Jarrett for the kind use of his pictures; John Pressley and David Roberts; John Allan; Chris Szypulewski for the kind use of his uncles 309 Squadron pictures; Kevin Marchbank for his kind help; Clive Braham.

Finally, a kind word for Amy Rigg at The History Press for her support, and also Katriona McCloskey for performing admirably the unenviable task of proofreading.

1

RENFREW AIRPORT

In common with many other towns and cities in Great Britain, there was considerable interest in aviation in the West of Scotland during the early part of the twentieth century. One event which drew large crowds was the *Daily Mail's* Circuit of Britain Air Race in July 1911 with prize money of £10,000. Starting from Brooklands, Paisley Racecourse was chosen as the Glasgow District landing ground and the event attracted a large number of spectators, estimated at 20,000. Coming from Stirling, the first arrival in his Bleriot Monoplane and eventual winner of the £10,000 was Frenchman Lieutenant Conneau flying under the name of 'Beaumont'. Another Frenchman Emile Vedrines got lost and had to land in Renfrew to get directions to the racecourse. Of the nine British competitors taking part, Colonel Cody was the only one to complete the course (although originally from Texas, Cody had been naturalised in 1909).

The year previous to this had seen the pioneering aviator James Radley demonstrate his Bleriot Monoplane at Lanark in June 1910, setting an unofficial new world speed of 75mph in the process. Another boost to aviation in the West of Scotland was provided in 1910 in the form of an aerodrome at Barrhead by the former honorary secretary of the Scottish Aeronautical Society, Walter G. Duncan, with two associates on the estate of G.H. Turner at Parkhouse, Barrhead. Two separate fires occurred at the aerodrome in 1911 and April 1912 with the second fire causing extensive damage, destroying a hangar and three aircraft.

The name of William Beardmore & Co. is closely associated with the start of aviation in Glasgow. The firm employed, at its peak, 42,000 people on Clydeside. Beardmore was named after its owner William Beardmore, Lord Invernairn, after whom the Beardmore Glacier in Antarctica is named. The company had a fairly diverse manufacturing base including aircraft, tanks, warships, naval armament, trains and airships. The First World War gave a major boost to Beardmore's aviation manufacturing and over 500 aircraft were produced at the Dalmuir factory.

There were three sites used for test flying by Beardmore: Moorpark Aerodrome, Dalmuir Aerodrome and Inchinnan Aerodrome. The R34 airship was built at Inchinnan and became the first 'aircraft' to fly the Atlantic both ways in 1919 and the first east to west crossing departing on 2 July and returning on 13 July 1919. Moorpark Aerodrome, which was eventually to become Renfrew Airport, started life as Moorpark Acceptance Aerodrome. There had been flying at Moorpark prior to its use as an air acceptance aerodrome. In 1913, James G. Weir was experimenting with flying in this area. A colleague of his from the Royal Flying Corps entered into negotiations with Renfrew Town Council and the tenants of the land between Newmains Farm and Arkleston Cemetery to lease the land for use as a flying field. The decision was taken in 1916 to create the facility at Moorpark, under the control of the Air Ministry, for testing of aircraft from Beardmore and other aircraft manufacturers including G. & J. Weir of Cathcart. In addition to its function as an aircraft acceptance aerodrome, it was also a maintenance and repair facility. However, before it reached its full potential, the First World War ended and by 1920 the aerodrome was deserted. It came back to life again in July 1923 when Beardmore were appointed to establish an RAF Reserve of Officers training school there. The new school was headed up by Mr A.J. Campbell, formerly of Beardmore's naval construction works at Dalmuir,

Beardmore BE2C and Wight 840 in production at Clydeside, 11 August 1915. The Wight 840 was originally designed and built by boatbuilder J. Samuel White on the Isle of Wight. (Courtesy of Philip Jarrett)

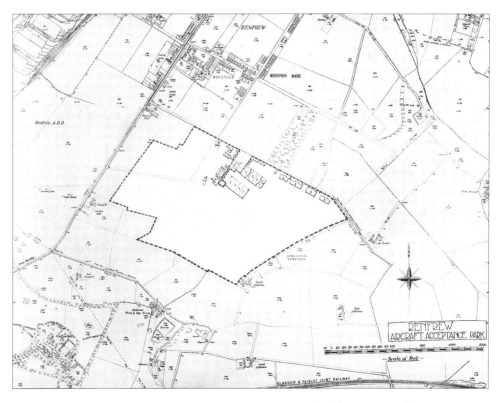

Renfrew Aircraft Acceptance Aerodrome layout. The aerodrome, which became virtually unused in the immediate post-First World War years, was to become Glasgow's first airport. (National Archive)

Launching a Wight 840 on the Clyde. Eleven of these versatile seaplanes were built at the Beardmore Works. (Courtesy of Philip Jarrett)

Airco DH9, built in 1918 by G. & J. Weir, being tested at Renfrew. Note the compass swinging pad, used to calibrate the aircraft's compass located in areas as free as possible from local magnetic disturbances. (Courtesy of Philip Jarrett)

and Captain A.N. Kingwill as chief pilot instructor. The school initially used three Avro 504Ks, one DH9 and one Bristol Fighter. The Avro 504Ks and the DH9 were fitted with dual controls for training purposes with the Bristol Fighter being used for more advanced training. The final test was a sixty-mile cross-country flight. Pilots appointed to the new reserve were formerly pilots in the Air Force and the three- to six-week training (dependant on weather and pilot ability) was basically a refresher course. The initial uptake of recruits was reported (surprisingly) as disappointing.

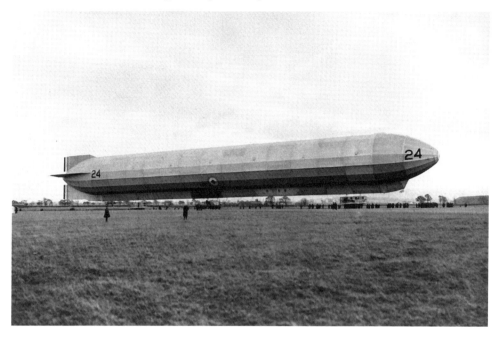

R24 Airship at Inchinnan. The R24 was the only one of two airships built of the R23 class under a contract awarded by the Admiralty to Beardmore. Among other functions she was involved in a series of severe weather tests in 1920 to help design a new mooring tower which could moor airships at wind speeds up to a maximum of 70 to 80mph. (Courtesy of Philip Jarrett)

The record-breaking R34 Airship at Inchinnan. The R34 was enormous at 643ft long. As with many airships, she was substantially damaged by bad weather in 1921, the useful equipment was removed and her remains were sold for scrap. (Courtesy of Philip Jarrett)

G-EARX Beardmore WB2B. (Courtesy of Philip Jarrett)

Handley Page V/1500 & Sopwith 2F1 Camel at Inchinnan. (Courtesy of Philip Jarrett)

After the war HP 0/400s flew newspaper flights and carried passengers for a short period, demonstrating the novel method of dropping newspapers by parachute over 1–12 May 1919 at various aerodromes including Moorpark. On 12 May HP 0/400 F5414, flown by Captain W. Shakespeare, crashed on take-off at Carlisle after a forced landing on the aircraft's return from Glasgow to Manchester.

Manchester Aviation Co. stationed an aircraft at Moorpark in July 1923 to operate an air taxi service for local businessmen. Aerial photography was also undertaken and the fares were calculated at 2s a mile.

Scottish Flying Club

The Scottish Flying Club was founded in 1927 with one DH60 Moth G-EBUU. A DH51 G-EBIQ was loaned to the club by the Chairman Air Commodore J.G. Weir. A second Moth G-EBVT was purchased in February 1928. The club proved to be popular and grew quickly. In November 1927, the club had 194 members. By May 1928 the number of members grew to 251 and by the end of 1928 it was 363. The club's instructor was Flight Lieutenant William Jones who had flown in the RFC during the First World War. He was succeeded by Captain John C. Houston in 1928. The president was the Right Honourable Lord Weir of Eastwood, with Harry W. Smith as club secretary. Despite almost inevitable accidents (with G-EBUU being the first casualty when it was written off in May 1928, replaced by a DH60 Moth G-EBYG in June 1928) the club continued to prosper. By 1931 the club had three DH60 Moths with a fourth being added in 1932. The SFC also had to contend with uncertainty over their lease on Moorpark. In 1933 the club negotiated a formal lease between itself and Renfrew Town Council. The SFC became the managers of the site for five years, with SMT and M and SAF as the main tenants of the hangars. Renfrew Town Council had taken over responsibility for the aerodrome from the Air Ministry some years previously.

In December 1933, the SFC started building a new clubhouse and headquarters at the aerodrome. The new building was constructed at the end of the easternmost hangar on the main site.

There were a number of changes to the club's personnel but it continued to thrive, producing the monthly magazine *Scottish Flyer*. In 1936 the chairman of the club was Air Commodore James G. Weir. In 1937, Flying Officer Alexander Wren replaced Captain Houston as chief instructor after the latter's unfortunate death as a passenger in Vega Gull G-AEWP on 3 July 1937 at Johnstone.

By the outbreak of war the club had a fleet of six Moth Majors, two Hornet Moths and two Tiger Moths. The SFC proved to be one of the main promoters of aviation in the West

John Houston, the chief flying instructor of the SFC, tragically killed in an accident in Vega Gull G-AEWP in which he was a passenger, on 3 July 1937. (Museum of Flight, National Museums of Scotland. Licensor: www.scran.ac.uk)

Beardmore Reserve School, Dalmuir, 23 December 1925. (Courtesy of Philip Jarrett)

The Scottish Flying Club engineering workshop at Renfrew 1933. (Courtesy of the Dugald Cameron Collection. Licensor: www.scran.ac.uk)

G-EBIG Airco DH9. A number of these former First World War light bombers were converted to carry passengers in the half-seat behind the cockpit. (Courtesy of Philip Jarrett)

of Scotland in the years before the outbreak of war and their treatment by the authorities afterwards left a great deal to be desired. Basically the airfield they had helped to promote was requisitioned at the start of the war and they were given no compensation for the loss of their bar, hangar and hotel. The club moved to Perth and ended up buying Couplaw Farm in the late 1950s. The club lost a number of members to the Glasgow Flying Club when they set up at Abbotsinch in the mid-1960s. After a relatively short but illustrious history, the SFC was eventually wound up in the mid-1970s.

The Scottish Flying Club hosting a public air pageant in 1934. The clubhouse seen here was to become the first terminal for Renfrew Airport. (Museum of Flight, National Museums of Scotland. Licensor: www.scran.ac.uk)

G-EBIS Avro 504K. The 504 series was the most produced aircraft of any kind that served in the First World War. The first flight of an Avro 504 took place in 1913, and by the time production ended in 1932 over 10,000 had been built. (Courtesy of Philip Jarrett)

G-EBOD Bristol Trainer Type 89A crashed close to a railway line in 1927. (Courtesy of Philip Jarrett)

Miles Hawk Trainer G-AKKY – one of four Miles Magisters (later converted) purchased by the Scottish Flying Club in 1952. Picture taken at Perth after the SFC was forced out of Renfrew. (Douglas Rough Collection)

John Cuthill Sword – Midland and Scottish Air Ferries (M & SAF)

There are a number of names associated with the establishment of aviation in Scotland. John Sword will always be remembered for having the vision and energy to establish the first airline services out of Glasgow at Moorpark Aerodrome and, in fact, these were the first airline services in Scotland. Born in Airdrie in 1892, he came to establish himself as a businessman with interests in a number of areas, principally running bus companies. By the end of the 1920s, his Midland Bus Services group had a network covering most of Scotland south and west of Glasgow. A far-sighted man with experience in aviation from the First World War, he saw the benefits of flying to the islands of Argyllshire and difficult terrain to the north and west of Glasgow, and the amount of time that could be saved by air travel to destinations in these areas.

He was heavily involved in the formation of the aviation division of SMT (Scottish Motor Traction Co.) in Fountainbridge, Edinburgh. SMT bought two DH83 Fox Moths (G-ABWB and G-ABWF) from Ted Hillman's Hillman Airways in Romford, Essex. Despite SMT being an Edinburgh based concern, G-ABWB was flown to Moorpark Aerodrome, Renfrew, from Romford and arrived after a four hour and ten minute flight on 2 July 1932, followed a couple of days later by G-ABWF. Shortly after their arrival, advertisements began to appear in the east and west of Scotland promoting air taxis at 1s per mile, carrying up to four passengers.

John Sword had worked closely with the SFC (Scottish Flying Club) at Moorpark Aerodrome. The SFC was leasing Moorpark from the Air Ministry and sub-leasing hangars they did not need for their own aircraft to other users. Both of SMT's Fox Moths were kept at the aerodrome as a base had yet to be established in Edinburgh.

Despite this promising beginning, Sword had other ideas. Taking Hillman Airways in the south as his guide, he wanted to establish regular scheduled air services. This was to lead to problems with the powerful directors of SMT.

By the end of 1932, John Sword was committed to starting his own airline independent of SMT. The first employee of his new airline was Harold Malet who had previously been SMT's chief pilot. He joined as chief pilot at Renfrew on 1 February 1933. An Airspeed Ferry G-ACBT was the first aircraft purchased and delivered on 8 February 1933. Sword had ordered a

A Beardmore 'Wee Bee' in 1924, which, despite being an unusual aircraft, won an Air Ministry prize of £2,000. Designed by the then youthful W.S. Shackleton, it flew at 78mph. (Courtesy of Philip Jarrett)

M&SAF Airspeed AS4 Ferry G-ACFB. The arrangement of the third engine being placed on the wing above the cockpit gave the pilot a better forward view. (Courtesy of Philip Jarrett)

second aircraft (DH Fox Moth G-ACBZ) which was also delivered to Moorpark Aerodrome on the same day. More Fox Moths and another Airspeed Ferry were ordered and operations grew quickly.

In early 1933, SMT had embarked on an expansion of their fleet by ordering seven more Fox Moths, giving it a total fleet of sixteen aircraft of various types.

On 10 March 1933, Sword officially registered his new Airline 'Midland & Scottish Air Ferries Ltd' (M & SAF) at the Company Registrar's Office in Edinburgh. He named himself as managing director and his wife Christina was the only other director. Amongst the new staff recruited was Scotland's first female pilot, Winifred Joyce Drinkwater. A remarkable woman, she had been a member of the Scottish Flying Club since 1930 and had gained her instructor's and commercial pilot's licenses as well as being a licensed engineer.

The airline concentrated on charter work and 'joyriding' initially and Sword leased part of one of the hangars at Renfrew Aerodrome from the SFC. The first scheduled service for the airline took place on 18 April 1933. Not only was this the first scheduled service for his airline, it was the first scheduled airline service in Scotland. Although the aircraft was carrying newspapers (*The Daily Express*), not passengers, from Glasgow to Campbeltown, the new service was a step in the right direction for Sword's vision. Passengers started to be carried on an ad hoc basis almost as soon as the service started.

On the third day of the service, DH Fox Moth G-ACCU flew from Renfrew to Campbeltown and then on to Islay. The aim was to develop services as quickly as possible to locations which required long transit times by surface transport. On 27 April, Winifred Drinkwater flew the Campbeltown service in DH Fox Moth G-ACBZ on her first scheduled flight and by so doing, becoming the first woman to fly a scheduled airline service in Scotland. In May 1933, M & SAF took delivery of no less than ten new aircraft including Avro X G-ACGF and DH84 Dragon 1s.

John Sword had placed a specially equipped DH84 Dragon (G-ACCZ) at the disposal of the Glasgow Area Hospitals to fly in seriously ill patients from inaccessible areas. In effect G-ACCZ became Scotland's first air ambulance, a service which has continued to the present day. The first patient to use the service was fisherman John McDermid, flown in from Islay on 14 May 1933 for a life-saving operation at the Western Infirmary, Glasgow. The ambulance service was later extended to cover the Mull of Kintyre, the Western Isles and eventually the Northern Isles.

Although Islay had been served from Renfrew via Campbeltown unofficially for a month, the service became official on 16 May 1933 after which Islay was served twice daily. The popularity of the service enabled John Sword to increase capacity on the route by the introduction of two of the larger eight-seat DH84 Dragons. The encouraging growth of the service prompted another extension. On 24 May 1933, the service was extended to include Rothesay, with Rothesay being the first stop on the outward journey to Campbeltown and Islay. However, Rothesay was only a 'call on demand' service which was not often used and it never enjoyed the popularity of the other two destinations.

An air pageant was held at Renfrew Aerodrome on 21 and 22 May 1933. These were always very popular events with the public and both M & SAF and SMT aircraft were there to give joy rides to the crowds.

A service from Renfrew to Belfast (Aldergrove) via Campbeltown, was started with the inaugural flight being flown by the Avro X G-ACGF on 30 May 1933. The new service, entitled 'The Irish Scot', operated twice daily (except Sundays) and attracted a good deal of attention from the business community in both cities.

On 3 June, the airline took delivery of a second Airspeed Ferry (G-ACFB) which was delivered to Renfrew from Airspeed's new factory in Portsmouth. As an interesting aside, the factory was owned by Neville Shute Norway (later to become better known as Neville Shute, the bestselling author).

By June 1933, Midland & Scottish Air Ferry aircraft were flying out from Renfrew to look at new landing grounds in the Western Isles including possible new destinations at Stornoway and Barra, although none of the sites and destinations looked at, came to fruition in the form of a scheduled service.

A new service was started on 12 July 1933 linking Hooton Park, Speke, the Isle of Man (Castletown) and Renfrew. This service was slightly more complex than a standard journey flying the route backwards and forwards from Hooton Park up to Renfrew and back. One part of the service started from Renfrew and flew to Castletown, while another aircraft left Hooton Park and went via Speke to arrive in time to coincide with the arrival from Renfrew. Passengers could then transfer aircraft to continue their journeys or disembark or join at Castletown if

M & SAF Airspeed AS4 Ferry G-ACBT at Renfrew. This was the first aircraft for John Sword's airline. The ferry had been designed to meet the requirements of Sir Alan Cobham, who wanted a pleasure flying airliner. Delivered on 8 February 1933, G-ACBT was dismantled in 1941. Seated on the left is Winifred Drinkwater. (Courtesy of Philip Jarrett)

that was their wish. From the first flights, the main source of revenue for the new service was early morning newspapers. The service from Renfrew to Castletown (dropped in 1933 and not restarted) carried early editions of the *Daily Record*, while the service from Hooton Park carried the early editions of English newspapers.

In 1933 10,000 passengers had already been carried by M & SAF. The winter of 1933/34 at Renfrew was spent concentrating on the routes already established and maintenance of the aircraft. Fares were also reduced over the winter to encourage passengers to continue using the services. Overhaul and maintenance of the aircraft could be a drawn out affair. For instance, DH Dragon G-ACDL took two months to get its certificate of airworthiness renewed at the aerodrome. Sword had radio equipment installed on two aircraft at a cost of £500 each and expressed the hope that the Air Ministry would grant him permission to establish a radio station at Renfrew. A powerful searchlight was used at Renfrew for night landings. The flight leaving Aldergrove Aerodrome near Belfast at 21.00 flying to Renfrew was able to pick out the beam of the searchlight ten miles from the Ayrshire coast.

One problem encountered by the M & SAF pilots was the confusion caused by the close proximity of Abbotsinch with aircraft mistaking the RAF base at Abbotsinch for Renfrew and landing there in foggy or murky conditions. It was a source of confusion that would continue right up until the closure of Renfrew Airport in 1966.

John Sword had announced that he expected a five-fold increase in passengers carried in 1934 to 50,000 and set about attempting to expand the airline to achieve this. He was good friends with Edward Hillman, who wanted to expand his air services centred on Romford in Essex, whilst John Sword wanted to expand his services centred on Renfrew and Liverpool. Thus the pair of them entered into a working relationship to achieve their respective aims. In particular, John Sword was looking to connect Renfrew with London and Paris, and both men were facing competition from rivals like London, Scottish & Provincial Airways.

An elegant new aircraft joined the fleet on 6 April 1934. This was Avro 624 G-ACFV, a sixteen seat, twin-engine airliner which was one of only two built. Just prior to this, amongst other services in the south, a new Hooton–Renfrew direct link was started (sometimes routed via the Isle of Man). Winnie Drinkwater flew the inaugural service from Renfrew to Hooton in Fox Moth G-ACCU with two passengers.

In a speech on Friday 6 April 1934 new services were announced for 1934. Using Liverpool as a hub, the main focus of the new services was the linking of Glasgow (Renfrew)–Liverpool (Speke)–Birmingham (Castle Bromwich)–London (Romford)–Paris (Le Bourget). Powerful competitors were now snapping at John Swords heels including Railway Air Services (RAS) and London, Scottish & Provincial (LS & P) were making plans for the trunk routes in Britain. LS & P had already flown an experimental flight to Renfrew from London (via Manchester and Nottingham) with an Airspeed Courier on 19 March 1934. KLM were also interested in serving UK regional airports from Amsterdam and had discussed this in 1933 with John Sword who had declined the offer as he did not have either the aircraft or the equipment at the time. KLM did, however, start operating a service to Speke from Amsterdam from June 1934 and these connected with M & SAF at Speke to take connecting passengers to Glasgow.

During the rest of April and May 1934, the airline operated its schedules without any problems. Winnie Drinkwater, previously mentioned, the sole M & SAF female pilot, had the distinction of being the first woman airline captain to fly a scheduled service between London and Glasgow, when she flew Fox Moth G-ACCU from Romford (acting as London airport on the schedule) to Renfrew via Speke on 28 May 1934. Renfrew Aerodrome had been approved for operation with full customs facilities by this time which enhanced the aerodromes status.

At the end of June 1934, John Sword was presented with an ultimatum by the railway directors of SMT which, in effect, was that if he wanted to continue as general manager of Western SMT then he had to cease his airline activities immediately or leave the group. The powerful directors were worried by his tie with Hillman Airways and the threat he posed to their aviation interests. Sword had little option but to comply. He had already put £80,000 of his money into M & SAF and estimated he had made a loss of half that amount (£40,000) to that

Another view of M & SAF Airspeed AS4 Ferry G-ACFB. This was the fourth model built and flew from Renfrew to Campbeltown, Belfast and Liverpool. Impressed into service with the RAF in 1941, it ended its days as an instructional airframe. (Courtesy of Philip Jarrett)

date. M & SAF had not had long enough to establish itself, but apart from that he faced powerful competition from other airlines like RAS (Railway Air Services) and London, Scottish & Provincial Airways who were going to compete on the main trunk routes. It must have been with a heavy heart that he wound the operation down. The Ambulance service for the Western Isles was retained with one aircraft (DH Dragon G-ACCZ) and the rest of the fleet was sold off. John Sword retained two of the aircraft for his personal use.

The services were stopped with the last Glasgow–London service being operated on 14 July 1934 and the Renfrew–Campbeltown and Islay services continuing a little longer until 29 September 1934.

So ended John Sword's contribution to the beginning of scheduled air services in Scotland. He had laid the groundwork for those who followed in his footsteps and one can only guess what this man of vision might have been able to accomplish, had he been allowed to do so.

Renfrew and Other Pre-War Commercial Operators

Northern Airlines began a Belfast–Renfrew service from 17 June 1924 operating from Malone aerodrome. However, the service was terminated after operating on an irregular basis due to weather problems.

Although they did not operate any scheduled services, Imperial Airways visited the aerodrome to give 'joy rides' at the Renfrew air pageants. Some examples were HPW8b G-EBBI over 5–7 June 1931, Westland IV G-AAGW in 1932, HP42s G-AAXC and G-AAXF in 1933 and AW15 Atalanta G-ABPI also in 1933.

SMT (Scottish Motor Traction) tended to concentrate on air taxi work, tuition, surveying and 'joy rides'. Although flying from a number of Scottish airfields and aerodromes, including Renfrew, they made their main base at Macmerry Aerodrome near Edinburgh. Towards the end of September 1933, SMT decided to run down their operations at Renfrew and sold their DH Dragon (G-ACDN) based there to John Sword on 22 September 1933.

In 1932/33, British Amphibious Airlines operated irregular charter services from Blackpool to Renfrew, Greenock and Rothesay using a Saunders Roe Cutty Sark G-AAIP. This was a four-seat amphibious aircraft and G-AAIP named *Progress I* was the prototype of only twelve built.

With Midland & Scottish Air Ferries out of the way in 1934, as previously mentioned, there were other companies waiting to step in to fill the gap. Railway Air Services (RAS) had started a service to Renfrew from London (Croydon) routed via Castle Bromwich, Manchester (Barton) and Belfast (Aldergrove) on 20 August 1934. The Belfast stop was moved to Newtownards on 31 August 1934. A Post Office contract was awarded to Railway Air Services for the route (operated with a DH86) which also started on the 20 August 1934. This was the start of their association with Renfrew which lasted until 31 January 1947. Railway Air Services started a Liverpool–Belfast–Renfrew service in November 1934. Hillman Airways had a previous connection with John Sword and they started their London (Essex Airport, Stapleford)–Liverpool (Speke)–Belfast (Newtownards)–Renfrew service on 1 December 1934. This meant that RAS and Hillman were competing directly with each other on the London–Renfrew service in 1935, albeit both from different London airports. Hillman's service was twice daily departing Essex at 10.00 and 14.00 with southbound flights from Renfrew departing at 08.30 and 16.10. The actual flying time was three hours and twenty-five minutes. On 30 September 1935 United Airways, Spartan Airways and Hillman Airways merged to form Allied British Airways Ltd, then dropping the name 'Allied' from the title on 29 October 1935 to become British Airways Ltd. They operated a Liverpool (Speke)–Blackpool (Stanley Park)–Isle of Man (Hall Caine)–Belfast (Newtownards) service with a connection to Renfrew departing from Newtownards within thirty minutes of arriving from the Isle of Man. The northern sector departed Speke at 10.15 and arrived at Renfrew at 13.40, which was good going considering there were three stops and one change of aircraft! The southbound leg, however, departed Renfrew at 07.50, but only went to Belfast's Newtownards Aerodrome, with much later connections. United Airways had operated a new service in 1935 from London (Heston) to Speke departing at 12.45 and arriving at Speke at 14.05 with a ten minute connecting time for a flight to Newtownards and Renfrew, with the ETA at Renfrew set at 16.40. The southbound leg of this daily (except Sundays) service departed from Renfrew at 14.15 and arrived at Heston at 18.10, again with a stop at Newtownards and a change of aircraft at Speke.

Highland Airways first commercial passenger aircraft G-ACEW, a GAL ST-4 Monospar MkII, early 1933. Sold to Mr Charles H. Tutt of London in March 1933, it was destroyed by fire at Croydon in December 1937. (Courtesy of the Dugald Cameron Collection. Licensor: www.scran.ac.uk)

Northern & Scottish Airways was formed by George Nicholson at Renfrew in 1934. The airline took over the Renfrew–Campbeltown/Islay services in the winter of 1934/35 starting a thrice-weekly schedule to Campbeltown on 1 December 1934 which was extended to Islay on alternate days. Northern & Scottish also took over the air ambulance service operating out of Renfrew. The airline also started a daily Renfrew–Isle of Man service with a DH84 Dragon which started on 17 May 1935. The service was three times a week but almost immediately became daily at the end of May 1935 and operated to Hall Caine Aerodrome (named after the Manx novelist) near Ramsey on the Isle of Man rather than Ronaldsway. On 1 July 1935 the service was increased to twice daily, and then reduced to a weekend only service in the winter of 1935/36. A Renfrew-Skye–North Uist–South Uist (Askernish)–Renfrew service was flown by Northern & Scottish. The South Uist segment had been extended from Skye in January 1936 and then to North Uist the following month. The round trip from Renfrew was operated in different directions on alternate days. From 10 June 1936 a connecting on-demand service from North or South Uist was offered to Barra and Benbecula and additionally from North Uist to Harris with a bus connection to Lewis. When Northern and Scottish merged with Highland Airways in 1937 to become Scottish Airways, Barra became a regular stop on the South Uist–Renfrew sector. Scottish Airways was also the operating company for Western Isles Airways.

On 14 January 1938 a Spartan Cruiser G-ACYK of Scottish Airways still carrying Northern & Scottish Airways titles crashed on the hill of Stake in the Largs Hills while carrying cinema film from Renfrew to Campbeltown. Both the pilot (Captain McGeevor) and the wireless operator escaped serious injury. The shell of the fuselage was removed by a Royal Navy Sea King helicopter in 1973 and taken to a nearby road where it continued its journey by road to the Museum of Flight at East Fortune.

A Renfrew–Belfast–Liverpool daily (except Sunday) service which was started by Northern & Scottish in 1936 operated until 1937 and was later continued throughout most of the war (as Scottish Airways) up to 1944. After the war started, all internal air services were suspended under the auspices of the AAJC (Associated Airways Joint Committee, set up on 5 May 1940 to oversee civil internal UK flights during the war). One of the first routes to be operated during the war was Glasgow–Campbeltown–Islay by Scottish Airways.

Prior to its merger with Northern & Scottish, Highland Airways (which had been started by another aviation pioneer, George Nicholson) had run a successful Renfrew–Orkney service in 1934.

Northern & Scottish Airways fleet, Renfrew 1937. (Museum of Flight, National Museums of Scotland. Licensor: www.scran.ac.uk)

Aberdeen Airways (owned by another pioneer of Scottish aviation, Eric Gandar Dower) flew a service from Aberdeen's Dyce Airport to Renfrew which started on 11 September 1934. The twice-daily service was flown by a Short Scion and a DH89 Dragon Rapide. During the winter the service operated only one flight (departing Dyce at 09.15 and returning at 15.45) on Wednesdays and Fridays when traffic justified the trip. Aberdeen Airways was renamed Allied Airways (Gandar Dower) Ltd with Eric Gandar Dower ploughing his own furrow until forced to hand his operation over to the heavy hand of the State after the war.

In September and October 1937, West of Scotland Air Services had looked at the possibility of operating a thrice-weekly Seaplane service from Greenock to Mull, Syke and Stornoway or Greenock, Portree, Tobermory and Stornoway, using their Scion Senior seaplane, and had looked at the possibility of using the former Harland & Wolff shipyard at Greenock as their base. In addition the director of West of Scotland Air Services, Captain Glyn Roberts, had visited Stornoway with two Air Ministry officials on 9 September 1937 to look at the use of the harbour in Stornoway for use by seaplanes. However, nothing came of this, possibly due to the fact that they faced competition to Stornoway from Highland Airways. Nonetheless, they did operate Short Scion G-ADDP on a Renfrew–Greenock–Arran (Shiskine) service from 1936 to 1938.

Another operator was Isle of Man Air Services which flew a service to Renfrew which started on 1 June 1938 and operated up to the beginning of the Second World War, recommencing from July to October 1946.

On 26 April 1938, it was announced by Provost Michie of Renfrew at a business lunch in Perth that there was a possibility of Renfrew closing down as a civil airport due to the unfairness of the Air Ministry in expecting a municipality to subsidise what should be a national service funded by central Government. This was not an argument confined to Renfrew. The catalyst for this came from the Scottish Flying Club's request for assurance from the Burgh of Renfrew that before renewing their lease, Renfrew would remain Scotland's sole southwest airport for some years. However, this guarantee could not be given and regrettably gave notice to the SFC that the lease would not be renewed. The Air Ministry made reference to Renfrew not meeting the requirement for a standard airport and suggested an airport serving

DH86A Express G-ADUE of Imperial Airways at Renfrew in 1937. On 8 November 1939, whilst flying between Hong Kong and Indo-China, G-ADUE was forced down on Waichow Island after being riddled with ninety-two bullets from Japanese fighters for straying too close to a military installation. She went on to serve in the RAF as AX762. (Museum of Flight, National Museums of Scotland. Licensor: www.scran.ac.uk)

both Glasgow and Edinburgh be situated midway between the two cities (i.e. Grangemouth). The matter was taken up in the House of Commons by the Marques of Clydesdale MP for East Renfrewshire, Neil MacLean MP and Sir Walter Smiles MP. This eventually prompted a telegram from the Air Ministry to Provost Michie guaranteeing a civil aerodrome at Renfrew for a period of two years, but that beyond that it was difficult to say owing to the restrictions on expansion at Renfrew. Earlier in April 1938 the Marques of Clydesdale had commented upon the 'dilly-dally' policy of the Government with relation to Renfrew and other civil aerodromes. Despite the two-year extension granted by the Air Ministry, the Second World War intervened.

Grangemouth and the Concept of a Central Scotland Airport (CSA)

On 13 February 1939, Scottish Aviation sent letters to both Edinburgh and Glasgow Corporations stating that they were preparing a facility and aerodrome at Grangemouth and put forward the suggestion that the aerodrome could serve both cities for civil flights. Although civil flights had already been operating from Renfrew, Turnhouse was still a busy military airfield with only occasional civil flights, and Edinburgh did not have an airport as such. Grangemouth Aerodrome was officially opened in July 1939. War was declared only two months later and the matter of a CSA serving Edinburgh and Glasgow was put to one side. However, neither corporation had seemed particularly interested in proceeding with the idea. A letter had been sent by Edinburgh Corporation to Scottish Aviation stating that they would send a delegation to discuss the matter with them, but there is no record of a meeting having taken place. Both cities appeared intent on developing their own airports. After the war Grangemouth was closed and Scottish Aviation moved to Prestwick with the area previously covered by Grangemouth Airfield being used to build the oil refinery which now stands there.

602 Squadron

602 (City of Glasgow) Squadron was formed on 12 September 1925 at Renfrew as a day bomber unit of the Auxiliary Air Force. It was initially equipped with DH9As. The squadron took delivery of its first aircraft, a DH9A trainer, on 7 October 1925. The facilities for the squadron were very basic to start with. Renfrew was a cramped aerodrome in terms of size and facilities (a recurring theme throughout the rest of its existence) and the squadron's town accommodation was a wooden hut within 52 (Lowland Division) Signals in Jardine Street before new premises were built at 49 Coplaw Street. From 1925 onwards, in common with other units of the Auxiliary Air Force, there followed fifteen years of constant change and re-equipment of the unit's aircraft. The DH9As were replaced with Fairey Fawns. The Fawn was a single engine light bomber, considered by many to be little better, performance wise, than the DH9A it had replaced. The view from the cockpit was also poor owing to the size of the large Lion engine. The Fairey Fawns were, in turn, replaced by Westland Wapitis in 1929. Hawker Harts then began to replace the Wapitis in February 1934 and they, the Harts, were then replaced in June 1936 with Hawker Hinds.

On 1 November 1938 602 Squadron was designated an army co-operation squadron, but changed on 14 January 1939 to become a fighter unit. 602 moved from Renfrew to the new airfield at Abbotsinch in 1933 and continued operations there until it started the first of many more moves throughout the war years, moving to Grangemouth in October 1939. The squadron achieved a distinguished war record and was involved in the shooting down of the first Luftwaffe aircraft of the war on 16 October 1939, when Junkers JU88s attacked Royal Navy warships in the Firth of Forth. Shortly after this, 602 Squadron Spitfires were involved in the shooting down of the first Luftwaffe aircraft on British soil (the earlier JU88s had crashed into the sea) on 22 October 1939. Known as the 'Humbie Heinkel' on account of it crashing

First parade of the newly formed 602 Squadron in 1925. (602 Museum)

First parade of the 602 Squadron pipe band in 1933. (602 Museum)

W. Scotland Aviation 13: G. & J. Weir of Cathcart built aircraft during the First World War. Then in the 1930s they moved into the new area of helicopter flight, building Autogyros like this Weir W2 in association with the Spaniard Juan De La Cierva. The only surviving example of the Weir machines is a W2 at the Museum of Flight, East Fortune. (Courtesy of Philip Jarrett)

This Weir W5 helicopter pictured at Cathcart in May 1938 was a modified version of earlier models. (Courtesy of Philip Jarrett)

near Humbie, Kidlaw, the Heinkel 1–11 was relatively intact and a machine-gun taken from it is on display in Edinburgh Castle. After the war, the squadron was disbanded in May 1945 at RAF Coltishall, reformed again at Abbotsinch in June 1946, and then moved over to Renfrew in June 1949 before finally returning to Abbotsinch in June 1954. After being equipped with Spitfire F21 and F22s after the war, 602 made the transition to the jet age when they re-equipped with Vampires and Meteor T7s. The end of an era came on March 1957 when 602 Squadron, along with the rest of the Royal Auxiliary Air Force, was disbanded. The squadron standard is now in Glasgow Cathedral. 602 Squadron was once again reformed on 1 July 2006 as a mission support unit with the task of supporting flying operations at RAF Kinloss and RAF Waddington. The squadron had been commanded by a number of distinguished officers over the years, including the Marques of Douglas and Clydesdale, Squadron Leader David McIntyre, Squadron Leader George Pinkerton, Squadron Leader Paddy Finucane and Squadron Leader Sandy Johnstone.

Renfrew and the Second World War

Renfrew started the war with the facilities provided by the Scottish Flying Club and four landing areas, the longest measuring 1,000 yards from east to west. Lockheed Corporation had established an aircraft assembly unit in the B1 hangars known as the Lockheed British Reassembly Division (later becoming part of the Lockheed Overseas Aircraft Corporation on 30 September 1943). The unit was exceptionally busy throughout the war as partially assembled aircraft were brought in by sea to the Clyde docks and transferred to the facility for full assembly, as well as other work being carried out on aircraft arriving by air. To give some idea of the throughput: from September to November 1943, there were twenty-three Douglas Boston IIIs and IIIAs arrived by air, and four Grumman Hellcats, ten Grumman Avenger IIs, twenty-six Grumman Martlets and fourteen Chance Vought Corsairs arrived by sea. During the same period the USAAF assembled four Lockheed P38 Lightnings, 361 P47 Republic Thunderbolts and forty-two North American Mustang P-51A and Bs. Lockheed's aircraft assembly work

309 Squadron:
double Browning
machine-
guns fitted
on a Westland
Lysander. (Chris
Szypulewski)

309 Squadron: the funerals of three airmen at Arkleston Cemetery with Renfrew Aerodrome in the
background. They died during the Luftwaffe raid on the night of 13 March 1941. (Chris Szypulewski)

309 Squadron: one of the squadron's Lysanders on patrol over the east coast of Scotland. (Chris Szypulewski)

was carried out under a succession of British Ministry of Aircraft Production contracts, which became a kind of 'reverse Lend-Lease' in that the value of the work in assembling aircraft for the USAAF was offset against the UK's Lend-Lease account with the USA.

On 6 November 1940, 309 (Polish) Squadron transferred over from RAF Abbotsinch with one Westland Lysander III T1467. The squadron took over one hangar plus other buildings and part of the former Scottish Flying Club premises became the officer's mess.

Squadron Leader Pistle was in command and Wing Commander NFW Mason of 11 OTU RAF Bassingbourn acted as his advisor. Although part of the Polish Air Force, the squadron was formed in order to act as part of the air wing of the Polish Army. All the new technical and flying personnel came from pre-war Polish units. It was equipped with second-hand Westland Lysander MkIIIs fitted with four machine-guns and light bomb racks. The two-seat Lysander was designed specifically as an army co-operation and tactical reconnaissance aircraft.

Full training began in October 1940 and consisted of low-level visual reconnaissance, picking up and delivering messages, artillery spotting, ranging and bombing. The squadron became fully operational on 11 November 1940. Its tasks were to patrol the Clyde Estuary and to keep two section aircraft on standby readiness against any German air invasion. With a top speed of 200mph the Lysanders were totally unsuitable aircraft to use in this latter interception role. The first operational flight of the squadron took place on 5 December 1940. There followed three fairly uneventful months until early March 1941 when German bombers attacked RAF Renfrew and caused extensive damage to the aerodrome and a number of casualties. Between 5 and 8 March 1941, German bombers attacked both RAF Renfrew and the city of Glasgow daily. The unit had commenced night flying training at this time, but during three night raids on Glasgow by the Luftwaffe on 12–14 March 1941, the squadron suffered a number of personnel killed or wounded. The unit was visited at Renfrew by President Raczkiewicz in April 1941 and was followed shortly after by HRH the Duke of Kent, accompanied by General Sikorski. On 15 May 1941, 309 Squadron was moved to Dunino Airfield near St Andrews.

Lysanders were again seen at RAF Renfrew when two Westland Lysanders of 116 Squadron were detached from Hatfield to RAF Renfrew, in early 1941, to be used to calibrate the anti-aircraft guns in placements near the airfield. Once their work was complete, the Lysanders moved on from Renfrew to Turnhouse and Ouston.

309 Squadron: a Westland Lysander undergoing maintenance. The aircraft in the background is most likely ex-M & SAF Avro Ten/Type 618 G-ACGF. (Chris Szypulewski)

309 Squadron: Lysanders carrying out exercises. (Chris Szypulewski)

Renfrew was closed from the summer of 1942 to May 1943, while two runways were constructed: 08/26 at 6,000ft long and 03/21 at 4,020ft long.

In 1943 Seafires, Sea Hurricanes and Swordfish started to arrive in addition to Grumman Martlets. Both the US Army and Air Force presence also grew and a wide variety of aircraft were soon covering the airfield including Douglas C-47s, Douglas A-20s, Boeing B-17 Flying Fortresses, Cessna UC-78 Bobcats, Bell Airacobras and later Consolidated B-24 Liberators. In addition to large numbers of these aircraft, newer and more secret aircraft also started to appear in 1944 such as the Northrop P-61 Black Widow and the Grumman F7F Tigercat. The Fairey Firefly Mk1 first visited on 2 September 1944. Another unusual aircraft to arrive for the first time in the summer of 1944 was a group of Vultee A-31 Vengeances for the RAF. The Consolidated B-24 Liberators which had started arriving in summer 1944 to have work carried out on them by Airwork for Far East operations, although other Liberators were to be seen from different units including Coastal Command. A group of Armstrong Whitworth

Aircraft like this Bell Kingcobra FR408 used Renfrew over Abbotsinch because of their high pressure tyres, which were unsuited to grass (as at Abbotsinch). There were only two British Kingcobras, both belonging to RAE Farnborough rather than the RAF. Kingcobra FZ440 (ex-USAAF 42-69423) flew from Renfrew to Farnborough on 20 September 1944. (Phil Butler)

KD152 Grumman F6F-5 Hellcat FII. One of eight visible on the apron by the Lockheed Aircraft Services hangar. (Tom McFadyen)

Albemarles arrived on 28 April 1945 and stayed for several months. Amongst all this military activity were the arrivals and departures of Scottish Airways Rapides and Dragons along with DH86s of Railway Air Services flying essential personnel and material around the country in particular with Scottish Airways to the Highlands and islands under the control of the Associated Airways Joint Committee.

The Renfrew Zero

One of the most unusual aircraft to pass through any airfield in the UK after the war appeared at Renfrew in April 1946. This was a Japanese Mitsubishi Zero A6M5 fighter. The interesting story behind this Zero was related by Captain Eric M. Brown CBE DSC KCVSA MA Hon FRAeS RN – more affectionately known as 'Winkle'. On 4 April 1946, whilst still a lieutenant-commander with Aero Flight at RAE Farnborough, he took off at 10.50 from RAE Farnborough for the one hour and forty minute flight to Abbotsinch in Grumman Tigercat TT349 (previously mentioned as one of two which passed through KGV/Renfrew/Abbotsinch on 8 December 1944). 'Winkle' had actually flown TT349 previously from Boscombe Down on 1 April 1946 to test a booster rudder. On arrival at Abbotsinch he left the engines running prior to making the short hop over to Renfrew where the Tigercat was to be made ready for shipment back to the USA. At Renfrew he left the Tigercat close to the old 'Belfast Truss' hangars near the control tower, assuming it would then be towed nearer to the Lockheed hangars which were closer to the docks. This area was generally full of aircraft-like Grumman Hellcats awaiting transit. It is believed also that the RN made use of a hangar at Renfrew for receiving and despatching aircraft.

Prior to leaving Farnborough, 'Winkle' had been briefed that there was a Zero at Renfrew and to get a look at it whilst he was there. Once he had finished with the Tigercat he asked some RN personnel if they knew of the Zero. He was shown the aircraft. On an as yet unknown date, an equally unknown ship brought the Zero into KGV where it was off-loaded and taken to Renfrew to await, it is believed, transhipment to the USA. The following day 'Winkle' watched US Navy personnel asking their RN counterparts for assistance in giving the Zero an engine run. Although he witnessed the engine run, he did not make himself known to the USN personnel. 'Winkle' heard that another engine run had been organised for the next day with only

A captured Mitsubishi Zero. This is not the A6M5 Zero flown at Renfrew by Lieutenant-Commander 'Winkle' Brown, but a similar type. Research has yet to reveal the fate of the latter Renfrew Zero. (Phil Butler)

RN personnel attending, presumably, he surmised, to allow the USN lads 'a run ashore'. That day, 4 April, before he departed for his overnight accommodation at Abbotsinch he asked the RN personnel if he could attend the engine run the following day and have a look at the Zero, to which they agreed.

On 5 April 1946 at around 16.00, 'Winkle' arrived by vehicle at Renfrew, by which time the Zero was outside ready for its engine run. This was carried out and the engine shut down. 'Winkle' observed the proceedings and then asked if they wouldn't mind if he gave the engine a run as well. There were no objections. Whilst sitting in the cockpit running the engine he shouted out to the RN personnel, 'I think I'll go a bit further than this!' With the engine running, he had acquainted himself with the cockpit layout which he said was all American instrumentation and that there were two data plates in English and Japanese. The English data plate identified the Zero as an A6M5 variant. He described the aircraft as having a scruffy grey-ish overall with no identity letters/numbers and with black (not red) US star/bar markings. There were lighter patches on the fin and forward fuselage which looked as though they had been painted over markings.

It was now approaching dusk and with nobody in the control tower he taxied out and took off at 17.20 for a forty-five-minute flight around the local area (i.e. no more than five to ten miles from Renfrew airport) thus ensuring he could return quickly to Renfrew in the event of a problem. He flew to 5,000ft and assessed the effectiveness of the controls, performing some aerobatic manoeuvres. Then, after a successful flight, he landed safely, taxied in and shut the engine down. After shut down he said to the watching RN personnel something along the lines of, 'You haven't seen this and don't mention it to the Americans!', or words to that effect. The Zero was put back into its hangar and 'Winkle' made his way back to Abbotsinch by vehicle, departing back to RAE Farnborough the next day in a Mosquito VI, RS657 flown by Squadron Leader Foster, CO of Aero Flight. 'Winkle' later wrote up his conclusions on the Zero for *Aero Flight*. He found it delightful to fly.

Very little is known about the identity of this Zero. It was believed to have come from the Far East, but no trace so far of its identity has been linked to Zeros known to have reached the USA.

However, there are believed to be approximately seventy Japanese ex-Second World War aircraft which arrived in the USA/UK and Canada which have still not been accounted for.

Renfrew Post-War

After the war, the 1946 Civil Aviation Bill gave BEA (British European Airways) sole responsibility for Domestic UK and European services. Not everybody was happy with this situation, but BEA progressed and absorbed all the UK airlines along with their routes, despite a proposal by Railway Air Services put forward before the war's end to develop and operate a comprehensive route network within the UK. The proposal was rejected but there was a transition period whereby some airlines were allowed to operate particular routes on behalf of BEA until BEA was in a position to fully operate the route on its own. For instance, Scottish Airways operated a number of services to the highlands from Renfrew including Renfrew–Tiree–Barra–Benbecula–Stornoway with DH89s in the summer of 1946 along with a thrice-daily service to Belfast (Nutts Corner) from February to July 1947 using DC3s. A feature of the Civil Aviation Bill was that BEA was required to establish Regional Advisory Councils starting with two for Scotland and one for Northern Ireland. The aim of these councils was to make BEA aware of regional needs, which was particularly important for Scotland as aviation was now starting to play a significant role, particularly in the more inaccessible parts of the country.

On 20 May 1946 a new age of commercial air travel came to Glasgow when Douglas DC3 G-AGYZ of Railway Air Services landed at Renfrew from Northolt and Prestwick before going on to Belfast. The DC3 would be a regular feature of airline operations at Renfrew just after the war and into the 1950s. On 18 November 1946, Railway Air Services commenced

Flygmoter Piper PA-23 Apache parked in front of Renfrew's control tower. SE-CBM arrived from Stavanger on 1 May 1961. (Gordon Reid)

a daily Northolt–Renfrew–Aberdeen service on behalf of BEA. Both Railway Air Services and Scottish Airways operated services from Renfrew on behalf of BEA. This was because, as already mentioned, BEA was unable to meet all its immediate commitments after its establishment as the national airline. One of the Scottish Airways visits nearly ended in disaster when JU52 G-AHOK (operating for BEA) arrived on 26 January 1947 and was promptly written off after its main wheels were damaged. The JU52 was a pre-war tri-engined German transport aircraft which had been used by the Luftwaffe during the war. G-AHOK was one of a batch of ten requisitioned by the RAF at the end of the war, reaching BEA via Railway Air Services and Scottish Airways. BEA gave the aircraft the class name of 'Jupiter' and they spent a considerable sum of money for the time (£12,500) modifying and refurbishing each one (the refurbishment work was carried out by Short Brothers and Harland of Belfast). The JU52s were used on Scottish internal flights from Renfrew to Inverness, Aberdeen, Orkney, Shetland and Stornoway. These aircraft were not very successful in Scotland as the only two airports which they could use with ease were Renfrew and Turnhouse, which both had ground power units. The lack of ground power units elsewhere meant the JU52/Jupiters had to leave one engine running after landing. If both engines had to be shut down, there would be a prolonged wait whilst a ground power unit was flown out from Renfrew to restart the engines. A severe lack of spare parts for these aircraft saw their withdrawal on 31 August 1947. The last service operated by the aircraft was a non-scheduled flight from Glasgow to Liverpool on the day they were officially withdrawn.

Renfrew was important to BEA as it was considered to be a main operating base for the airline along with Northolt at the end of the 1940s and beginning of the 1950s. A BEA route network map of August 1947 shows Glasgow serving all the Scottish Civil airports and airfields including Prestwick and Turnhouse along with flights to Belfast, the Isle of Man, Liverpool, Manchester and Northolt. There were thirteen flights a week between Northolt and Renfrew. BEA also established an international service along with the first recorded visit of a Vickers Viking on 12 August 1947 when G-AIVC of BEA inaugurated a new Copenhagen–Croydon–Renfrew service. The first flight by G-AIVC actually flew direct to Glasgow from Copenhagen.

BEA Pionair Leopard G-AHCX in the BEA Engineering Hangar. She was sold to Yemen Airways in 1962. (Colin Lourie)

This was a three-times-a-week service but passenger loads were poor and the route was abandoned on 1 December 1947. Another milestone was the start of a new service on 29 July 1947 from Dublin by Aer Lingus using DC3s. This was the first scheduled service by a foreign airline.

In the summer of 1947, BEA ordered five helicopters from the USA and formed a Helicopter Experimental Unit. The first public appearance of BEA's helicopters took place in Glasgow at Hampden Park on 28 September 1947 when two Sikorski S51 helicopters (G-AJOR and G-AKCU) gave demonstrations of their capabilities.

The poor financial position of BEA in the winter of 1947/48 saw the suspension of the daily Isle of Man–Renfrew service. This was one of many cost-cutting measures by the airline but BEA did reinstate the service in the summer of 1948 unlike a number of other routes which had been dropped permanently that winter. Despite the attempts at economy in the winter 1947/48 schedules, BEA reduced fares on a number of Scottish internal routes in order to stimulate passenger growth. Part of the problem on many routes served out of Renfrew was the fact that traffic densities were low, particularly with the Rapide services. In fact, 20 per cent of BEA's losses at the time were on domestic routes in Scotland. In a further effort to build traffic, BEA increased the frequency on the Northolt–Renfrew service on the summer schedules which started in April 1948.

By virtue of being one of BEA's two main operating bases, Renfrew was chosen to undertake DC3 maintenance which had previously been carried out at Liverpool's Speke Airport. BEA maintenance had been split over a number of locations and the main problem with maintenance of the DC3s at Speke was that the aircraft had to go there empty which added considerably to costs. This problem did not arise at Renfrew where far more services operated. The transfer from Speke to Renfrew was undertaken between 3 January and 24 March 1949, but it was not until the following year that the major DC3 maintenance dock was brought into use. The BEA maintenance facility used the B1 hangars vacated by Lockheed at the end of the war.

The concept of an air ambulance service for the Highlands and Islands which had been started in 1933 was continued by BEA. The airline established a special Air Ambulance Unit at

Renfrew in April 1948. BEA had provided an air ambulance service since February 1947 and operated 182 ambulance flights up to the establishment of this dedicated unit. Consisting of two Rapides, the unit was managed by Captain David Barclay and comprised three pilots and three radio officers. The unit was on call twenty-four hours a day, 365 days a year, and whilst there were difficulties with provision of the service to some locations, nonetheless the unit provided an invaluable service to the remote communities.

BEA Vickers Viking G-AIVE Crash 21 April 1948

If an aircraft crash can ever be said to have a happy ending then the crash of BEA Vickers Viking G-AIVE on the evening of 21 April 1948 was one. There were no fatalities despite the aircraft being written off.

The Viking was on a routine commercial flight from Northolt to Renfrew with sixteen passengers and four crew on board. The crew consisted of Pilot Captain John Ramsden, Co-Pilot Denis Clifton, Radio Officer Arnold Lloyd and Con Moroney the steward. John Ramsden lived at Newton Mearns and had flown Dragon Rapides out of Donibristle. Incidentally, Denis Clifton would be involved in another near disaster fourteen years later in September 1962, as captain of a BEA Vickers Vanguard which hit a flock of seagulls as it was taking off from Turnhouse. This caused a loss of power in two of the four engines, but he was able to steer the stricken Vanguard back to safety and disaster was averted.

The Viking was preparing to land at Renfrew when it came down in moorland in the Ayrshire Hills on the northern slope of Irish Law at 1,587ft. Miraculously only relatively minor injuries were sustained: a male passenger received a head wound and a broken ankle was suffered by passenger May Most of Kilmarnock Road, Glasgow, who was travelling with her daughter Hilda. Although the aircraft burst into flames, the passengers were able to escape through a gap torn in the rear fuselage. Then, splitting into three groups, the survivors made their way to safety in atrocious weather.

The first group consisted of the captain, twenty-eight-year-old John Ramsden and passenger Henry Watt (a company secretary of Drumchapel). They set out across the hills and reached Largs three hours later. Another group consisting of three male passengers led by the plane's radio officer also trekked for three hours at daybreak before reaching Ladyland House near Kilbirnie – home of Sir Neil Cochrane-Patrick.

The remainder of the party, including Mrs May Most who had to be carried because of her broken ankle, eventually reached Flatt Farm, Largs. A fleet of taxis and ambulances took them to a local hotel.

Another BEA Vickers Viking crash in 1948 also involved Renfrew. On 6 January 1948, Viking G-AHPK was on a routine commercial flight from Renfrew to Northolt (the reverse route to G-AIVE) with fourteen passengers and a crew of four. After a number of failed approaches to Northolt airport in poor weather, the aircraft hit some trees and crashed in a field at Ruislip. Unfortunately there was one fatality.

The 1950s

For its summer schedule in 1950, BEA started another international route out of Renfrew. This was a weekday service to Paris via Manchester operated by a DC3 which started on 28 April 1950. Another new service started by the airline was Renfrew to Perth, a daily service running from Mondays to Saturdays and operated by Rapides. The service started on 1 July 1950 but was discontinued on 31 August 1950 due to very poor loads. One of the reasons put forward for the low passenger figures was the fact that it was a midday service which had poor connections at Renfrew southbound which were morning and evening flights.

Dan Air Avro York G-ANTI, leased by BEA to operate their Heathrow–Manchester–Glasgow cargo
service prior to taking delivery of their Argosys. (Colin Lourie)

On 1 August 1950 the prototype Vickers Viscount G-AHRF arrived at Renfrew for the first
time. Arriving in the then new BEA colours, the Viscount represented a new breed of post-war
airliners and would be seen in large numbers in later years at both Renfrew and Abbotsinch.
When it arrived at Renfrew G-AHRF had just entered the history books a few days previously
when it made the first ever scheduled flight by a turbine-powered aircraft on 29 July 1950 from
Northolt Airport to Le Bourget, Paris.

On 1 June 1950 a proving flight for an unusual form of air travel took place when Short
S25 Sunderland MkIII G-AGJN arrived on the River Clyde. This was one of twelve aircraft
originally operated by BOAC and named Hythe Class. The flying boat of Aquila Airways
had landed on the River Clyde at Greenock after the short trip from Albert Dock at Leith.
Amongst the passengers was the managing director of Aquila Airways, Barry Aikman who
was keen to promote the flight as the start of the first inter-city flying boat service in
the UK. There were two routes from Southampton, the first to Edinburgh (Leith) and the
second to Glasgow (Greenock). The service to Greenock officially started on 4 July 1950
with a Short Sunderland taking just over two hours to complete the journey. The frequency
was one flight a week with the round trip from Southampton to Glasgow being flown on
Tuesdays and Southampton to Edinburgh being flown on Fridays. The fares were set at £9
single and £16 4s return which were comparable to the first-class rail fares between the
respective cities at the time. The single fare was slightly less than the comparable first-class
rail fare with a sleeper and the return fare was slightly more than a first-class return although
the air tickets were valid for a period of six months from the time of issue. At the time of
the proving flight Barry Aikman had stated that an increase in frequencies would depend on
demand, but unfortunately passenger figures proved to be very poor and the services to both
Glasgow and Edinburgh were abandoned almost as soon as they started, incurring heavy
losses.

In the summer of 1951, BEA started a new seasonal summer service direct to Jersey from
Renfrew with Pionairs. Pionairs were BEA DC3s which had been converted at a cost of
£10,000 per aircraft to include new seating, built-in air stairs, a replacement of cockpit equipment plus other modifications to upgrade the aircraft. At the time of the opening of the new
Jersey–Renfrew route, BEA introduced another low fare initiative on their Channel Island

A DH82A Tiger Moth converted to a Jackaroo G-AOIT. On 2 March 1960 Captain J. S. Swanson started an inter-Orkney air taxi and air ambulance service using this aircraft on unprepared strips provided in the most part by farmers. He was unable to continue the service as no Government subsidy or support was forthcoming. (Colin Lourie)

flights. These off-peak fares offered a 25 per cent reduction on midweek flights on virtually all routes but not on the direct flights to Jersey from Glasgow.

BEA's Rapides were withdrawn from service on Scottish routes on 1 October 1952 and replaced by Pionairs. The Renfrew–Campbeltown–Islay and Renfrew–Tiree services were henceforth served by the larger capacity Pionairs. Pionair G-AGIU operated the first service to Campbeltown and Islay whilst Pionair G-ALXL operated the first service to Tiree. Part of the problem with the introduction of the Pionair was the increased capacity on already low-density routes. Tiree could not justify a service in its own right from Renfrew with the larger aircraft so it became a stop on the Renfrew–Benbecula–Stornoway service. However, despite the upgrade of equipment on Scottish services, BEA sold nine of their Rapides, retaining three at Renfrew for the Air Ambulance Service and the Barra Service. Renfrew to Barra still had to be operated by a Rapide as the Pionairs could not land on the beach at Northbay.

In 1952, the Commercial Department of BEA set out to increase domestic passenger traffic on a number of routes by offering cheaper fares. The London to Glasgow and Edinburgh trunk routes were quieter at weekends and a new cheap weekend return fare of £8 was offered on both routes in an effort to increase passenger numbers. The cheaper fares were successful and figures were boosted on both routes at the weekends. BEA also opened a new sales office in Glasgow at the same time.

The opening of the large new BEA maintenance facility (for the new Viscounts and Ambassadors coming into service) at Heathrow in March 1952 involved the transfer of maintenance facilities for the Viking from Northolt to Renfrew. This transfer took place in March and April of that year and was a relatively short-term measure as the BEA Vikings were scheduled to be withdrawn from service by the end of 1954. The number of BEA engineering staff based at Renfrew had grown to 700 by 1954. As previously mentioned, Pionair maintenance was already being carried out at Renfrew and a new maintenance dock for this aircraft was opened on 13 October 1952. However, the same problem which had occurred at Liverpool's Speke Airport was now starting to occur at Renfrew, namely that many Vikings and Pionairs were positioning for maintenance empty which was adding to costs. This was particularly the case

N992 Douglas DC 6B owned by Reynolds Metal Co. (Colin Lourie)

A Tradair Viking G-APOR. Tradair ran into financial difficulties and was taken over by Channel Airways in 1963. (Iain Mackay)

for aircraft operating Channel Islands routes and within Germany. Wherever it was possible, aircraft requiring maintenance were scheduled to operate services into Renfrew.

Aer Lingus introduced the Bristol Freighter on their Dublin route with EI-AFS being the first of the type to visit Renfrew in 1953.

Another first was the operation of a scheduled London–Glasgow service by BEA Viscount G-AMOB on 17 July 1953. Viscounts were starting to be introduced on a number of BEA's routes, particularly to Europe but they were only occasionally seen on the London–Glasgow route for some time as BEA wanted to use the passenger pleasing Viscount on European routes where they were in competition with national airlines.

Although in 1954 a direct service from Glasgow to Southampton was still some years away (except the shortlived Aquila Airways flying boat service), an innovative way of travelling between the two cities was introduced via Heathrow and Northolt. A helicopter from the BEA Helicopter Experimental Unit flew a single round trip each day to connect with flights to and from the London airports to Glasgow, Edinburgh, Aberdeen, Belfast and a number of European destinations. The helicopter used was the Bristol 171, with G-AMWH flying the inaugural service. The Bristol 171 was replaced by the Westland WS55 later in 1954. However, the service was uneconomical and was abandoned the following year.

Air Safaris HP
Hermes G-ALDT
on 1 July 1961. (Iain
Mackay)

An Aviameer Airlines
Vickers Viking 1B
OO-EEN. Aviameer
was formed in 1958
and undertook
European charter
flights from their
Antwerp base. The
airline ceased trading
after just two years,
and its only aircraft,
seen here at Renfrew
on 15 May 1960, was
scrapped at Southend
in 1962. (Iain Mackay)

In 1954 BEA was looking for additional ways of boosting passenger figures and decided to extend its luxury first-class services to other routes from its lunchtime Silver Wing London–Paris service. The London–Glasgow service was known as the Clansman Service and operated from London to Glasgow in the evening, returning the following morning. None of these luxury services were particularly successful in boosting numbers, and by March 1960 they had all been discontinued, including the Clansman Service.

An era passed on 30 October 1954 when all civil operations were transferred from Northolt over to Heathrow. There were six flights that day from Northolt to Renfrew and three flights in the opposite direction. From the following day all flights from Renfrew to London were to Heathrow. October 1954 also saw the withdrawal of the Vickers Viking from BEA service

A new service to from Renfrew to Newcastle and Paris Le Bourget was started by Hunting-Clan Air Transport on 14 April 1954 with DC3 G-AMSK flying the first service. Hunting-Clan was formerly Hunting Air Travel which had been wholly bought by Clan Line, itself part of a large shipping conglomerate. The new owners had ambitious plans for the airline and amongst the plans were six flights a week between Renfrew and Newcastle's Woolsington airport starting in the summer of 1954. The schedule was Newcastle to Renfrew on Tuesdays, Thursdays and Saturdays leaving Newcastle at 17.15 and arriving at Renfrew an hour later at 18.15.

The return flights were flown on Mondays, Wednesdays and Fridays leaving Renfrew at 10.15 and arriving at Newcastle at 11.15.

Hunting Clan's Vikings were mainly used on the route but DC3s were sometimes used on the Newcastle to Renfrew flights on Thursdays and Saturdays and Mondays and Fridays in the reverse direction. In addition to the Le Bourget service from Glasgow, an effort was made by Hunting Clan to promote connections from Newcastle. With the arrival of the aircraft at 10.15 at Newcastle, a passenger from Glasgow could take a connecting flight on Mondays and Fridays to Amsterdam and Dusseldorf on a Hunting Clan Viking, departing at 11.15. The return sector was flown on Tuesdays and Saturdays arriving at Newcastle at 16.30 and departing for Renfrew at 17.15, arriving there at 18.15. In addition to this there was also what was advertised as 'Special Tourist Services' in the airline's schedules. These special tourist services were two separate services for passengers connecting at Newcastle from Glasgow and Manchester (the Amsterdam and Dusseldorf service just mentioned was for Manchester flights as well as for Glasgow). The first was a connecting flight at Newcastle to Hamburg and Copenhagen on Mondays at 11.00 (the flight from Renfrew arriving at 10.15), returning to Newcastle on Tuesdays at 16.40 and departing to Renfrew at 17.15. The second service was a connecting flight at Newcastle to Stavanger and Oslo with passengers again arriving from Renfrew at 10.30 and departing at 11.15 on Wednesdays. The return sector was flown on Thursdays, arriving back to Newcastle at 16.30 with the connecting flight departing to Renfrew at 17.15.

Hunting Clan used their Vikings to operate both of these special tourist services. Unfortunately, passenger numbers did not reflect the airline's optimism and despite every effort which had been made to promote the Newcastle–Glasgow sector of these routes and keep connecting times at Newcastle to a minimum, the Newcastle–Renfrew route was taken over by Dragon Airways, a small airline which had been bought by Hunting Clan (along with Elder Dempster and Tyne Tees Shipping), on 1 November 1955, to take over their Northern network of routes and to operate all former Hunting Clan services out of Newcastle – now the new base for Dragon having moved from Liverpool. Dragon Airways used their DH Herons on the Renfrew–Newcastle route in place of the larger DC3s and Vikings operated by Hunting Clan. Dragon Airways had started life in 1953 operating pleasure flights for Butlins at Pwhelli from Broomhall Airfield. They were already operating the Liverpool (Speke)–Renfrew service which they had gained permission for in June 1954 but only started operating a four-days-a-week service from 28 June 1955, for which they used Dragon Rapides G-AIYP, G-AHPT and G-AKOB. These were later replaced on the Liverpool route by DH Herons ordered in 1955 with G-ANYJ delivered in May and G-ANCI delivered in June 1955, followed by G-AODY in December 1955. G-ANYJ was mainly used on the service which was year-round and in June

Silver City Bristol 170 G-AIFM on 1 July 1961. This aircraft appeared in the 1957 film *The Man in the Sky* starring Jack Hawkins. The real star of the film, however, was the Bristol 170 G-AIFV. (Iain Mackay)

1955 operated the Glasgow Hunting Clan services to Newcastle. In June 1956 Dragon purchased Viking G-AOCH from Fields. The Viking was used on the same routes as the Herons where the loads were too heavy for the Herons. The Glasgow–Liverpool (Speke) route ceased in June 1956. For the rest of 1956 into early 1957 Dragon Airways continued to lose money before being taken over by the British Aviation Services Group and becoming part of Silver City's Northern Division.

On 26 November 1954 Renfrew's new terminal building was opened by J. Boyd Carpenter, the Minister of Transport and Civil Aviation. Designed by William H. Kininmonth of Edinburgh in an Art Deco style, it was a vast improvement on the old facilities. The first passengers to use the new terminal arrived from Barra on a BEA Dragon Rapide shortly after the official opening.

Since it was started in the summer of 1951, the Channel Islands service to Jersey was proving to be popular and was building on this success; BEA also started a new Renfrew–Guernsey service on 4 June 1955 using Pionairs.

The three BEA Rapides operating the air ambulance service and the Renfrew–Barra service were finally replaced in 1955. Two de Havilland Heron 1Bs were delivered to Renfrew and in a special ceremony on 18 March 1955, G-ANXA and G-ANXB were named Sir John Hunter and Sir James Turner (both medical pioneers) respectively. The guests at the ceremony were then treated to a flight in the aircraft.

Maitland Air Charters Super Aero 45S G-APRR on 11 November 1959. Note the tail of Ilyushin IL 14 OK-BYO in the background. G-APRR was still going strong up until 28 February 2009 when she crashed on take-off at Blackbushe. The aircraft was badly damaged and her future is currently uncertain. (Iain Mackay)

Derby Aviation Miles Marathon 1A G-AMHR on 5 May 1959. Purchased in 1955 along with G-AMGW from West African Airways Corporation, they were the only two British-registered civil passenger-carrying Marathons. (Iain Mackay)

The Herons were used initially on a weekday morning service to Tiree which saw the with-drawal of BEA's Pionairs on this route which had been served on the Benbecula service with the larger Pionair which did not justify the loads carried to Tiree. The Herons flew first to Tiree before going onto Barra and then making the return journey, again via Tiree. The Herons were able to operate into Barra's unique beach 'airport' which could only be used when the tide was out! Occasionally the Herons flew an evening service over the route. This schedule during the summer was reduced to three return flights a week in winter.

G-ANXB flew the first Heron ambulance flight on 4 March 1955 with the aircraft starting passenger services on 1 April 1955 when the Rapides were officially withdrawn from service and sold off by BEA. The BEA Herons were to become a strong symbol of Glasgow's links with the Highlands and Island communities they served, probably more so than any other aircraft used on these routes. The two aircraft were joined by a third Heron 1B in 1956 when G-AOFY (this registration was originally allocated to a DC6A but was not taken) joined the airline at the beginning of the summer 1956 season.

BEA had an unfortunate incident when their Viscount G-AMOA landed on 12 December 1955. The Viscount left the runway too fast and the right-hand undercarriage snapped off.

The hills near Largs claimed another aircraft on approach to Renfrew on 28 March 1956 when a Douglas DC3 G-AMRB of Starways was making an instrument approach to the aero-drome. It hit Greenside Hill at 1,250ft. The aircraft was on a positioning flight from its base at Liverpool's Speke Airport to operate a flight the following day from Renfrew to Lourdes. As the aircraft was on a positioning flight there were no passengers on board but the co-pilot was killed in the crash. The captain pulled the air hostess clear and despite having severe injuries went to raise the alarm before returning to the crash site. On arrival the fire brigade were unable to run their hoses to the crashed aircraft and had to use hand-carried extinguishers instead, which proved ineffectual. Starways were a Liverpool-based airline but operated charter flights from Glasgow to Spain, France and Switzerland. The crashed DC3 was positioning for just such a flight.

By 1958 the Starways fleet comprised of three DC3s and two DC4s. They had also started operating a scheduled flight from Renfrew to Jersey which BEA had flown since 1951.

BEA was always looking at ways of improving the services to the Highlands and Islands. In 1956 they introduced a new service to Benbecula from Renfrew. This was an evening service on Mondays, Fridays and Saturdays using Pionairs. Unfortunately the service was not a great success and was dropped in 1958.

On the engineering side, in 1956 BEA transferred major Pionair maintenance from Renfrew to the new facility at Heathrow between June and August. All major maintenance for BEA

Aviaco Douglas DC 6B EC-ASR on 15 June 1962. This DC 6 had been leased from Sabena in 1962/63 and went on to the West German Air Force as CA+023 in 1965. (Iain Mackay)

aircraft was now undertaken at Heathrow with the exceptions of the Rapides which were maintained at Jersey and the Two Herons at Renfrew. However, there was severe pressure on the BEA engineering base at Heathrow and it was decided to improve the facilities at Renfrew so that maintenance could be carried out on Viscounts there (along with Manchester) to ease the pressure at Heathrow.

On a more positive note, the London–Glasgow route was BEA's busiest in terms of passenger numbers. In the year 1954/1955 92,347 passengers were carried. This increased to 133,087 in 1956/1957, almost 24,000 more than their next busiest route from London to Belfast. In fact, London–Glasgow would remain the busiest domestic route for many years to come. BEA had started to take delivery of their new V802 series Viscounts in early 1957 and the first commercial flight of a series V802 to Renfrew was with G-AOJD arriving from Heathrow on 13 February 1957 with forty-seven passengers.

The year after the crash of the Starways DC3 near Largs saw another tragedy linked to Renfrew. On 28 September 1957 G-AOFY which had only joined the other two BEA Herons the previous year left Renfrew on an air ambulance call to Islay to pick up a patient from Port Ellen who required urgent attention. It was night-time and the weather was atrocious with very low cloud and rain restricting what little visibility there might have been in the darkness. As the Heron turned onto finals for landing, its left wing struck the ground and the aircraft crashed killing the three occupants of the aircraft including Sister Jean Kennedy. The subsequent accident investigation concluded that the Heron had lost considerable height and that the pilot had been attempting to concentrate on visual references in the appalling visibility and darkness in order to attempt to land and had not appreciated how much height the aircraft had lost. The report also concluded that due to the urgency of the ambulance flight the pilot probably decided to attempt to make a landing when in other circumstances he may have decided to abandon the attempt. Nevertheless, it was a tragic loss and BEA did not replace the aircraft. This loss was reflected in the schedules flown by the remaining Herons. Prior to the accident BEA had attempted to improve the Highlands and Islands flights by positioning one of the Herons at Stornoway from Renfrew in order to fly an early morning service: Stornoway–Inverness–Renfrew. At lunchtime it then flew a Renfrew–Inverness–Wick sector before finally flying a Renfrew–Inverness–Stornoway service. The early morning and evening flights were popular with passengers from Inverness and Stornoway as they enabled them to spend a full day in Glasgow and return in the evenings. After the loss of G-AOFY, the remaining two Herons returned to operating the six days a week from Renfrew to Tiree and Barra in the summer season, along with the continuation of the air ambulance service. The winter schedule for the Herons was five flights a week to Tiree from Renfrew and three weekly to Barra. This schedule for the Herons remained in place for the next eleven years.

Balair Vickers Viking HB-AAN 1B. This Viking was used to bring fans in for the football match on 17 May 1960; a practice which has continued throughout the years with the numbers of fans and aircraft getting larger and larger.
(Iain Mackay)

Air ambulance requirements took up much of the two Herons work. There were on average 250 air ambulance flights a year carrying approximately 300 patients. The Western Isles and Islay formed the bulk of the flights but there were occasional flights to Orkney and Shetland with the patients from the Northern Islands going to Aberdeen and those from Islay and the Western Isles going to Glasgow for treatment. Occasionally some flights from the Western Islands would take patients to Inverness. The cost of operating the air ambulance service was £12,000 per annum. A sum which was provided by the Scottish Health Service as opposed to the usually (in its early days at least) cash-strapped BEA. The Herons on air ambulance duty carried two stretchers and a nurse from a Glasgow hospital. The nurses always received extra training to familiarise themselves with the medical equipment carried on the Herons.

Derby Aviation, later to become Derby Airways (the forerunner of British Midland Airways) began services to Glasgow from Burnaston Airport near Derby in 1956 using Miles Marathons, amongst other aircraft on the route including a DC3 which had been had been converted from ex-RAF C-47B KN628 and given the civil registration G-AOGZ. This aircraft had been the personal aircraft of Field Marshall Montgomery whilst in RAF service. Rolls-Royce used the daily Derby–Glasgow service extensively which guaranteed a certain passenger load on the route for Derby Aviation/Airways. Apart from the Rolls-Royce link because of the factories in Derby and Scotland the airline had also been contracted by Rolls-Royce to fly their engines worldwide from Burnaston Airport.

Glasgow has had a long aviation link with Iceland. Flugfelag Islands/Icelandair, the Icelandic airline first started flying into Renfrew in 1948. Prior to this Scottish Airways had operated services on their behalf using Liberators from Prestwick before Flugfelag Islands/Icelandair took over and the Copenhagen–Glasgow–Reyjavik service was eventually transferred from Prestwick to Renfrew at the start of the summer schedule in 1955. The first flight was on 15 May 1955 (delayed by one week due to a strike in Iceland) and the service was twice weekly with one flight going on to Heathrow and the other to Copenhagen. The airline initially used DC4s TF-ISE and TF-IST on the route. Flugfelag Islands/Icelandair introduced Viscounts TF-ISN and TF-ISU on this route from 17 November 1958 with the frequency being increased to four flights a week. Both sectors of the routes to Copenhagen and Reykjavik proved to be very popular for many years with Scottish businessmen and tourists and payloads were consistently high.

In October 1956 Loftleidir/Icelandic Airlines introduced low fare flights through Renfrew. At first this was only on the westbound leg from Stavanger but was later changed on some of

Augusta Bell AB-47G Italian Air Force MM80131 on 11 April 1958. It arrived the previous day from Elmdon via Speke to demonstrate its capabilities to BEA and the Scottish Air Ambulance Service. (Douglas Rough)

the early services to Luxembourg. The weekly low-cost service, which routed Luxembourg–Glasgow–Reykjavik–Goose Bay–New York grew to be very successful. In May 1957 Loftleidir started services to Heathrow via Renfrew. The eastbound leg was flown on a Wednesday with the return sector flown on a Thursday. As previously mentioned, Loftleidir also started serving Luxembourg via Renfrew once a week, also in May 1957. This was a seasonal summer service. The eastbound service was flown on Saturdays with the return on Sundays using DC4s LN-HAT, TF-RVH, TF-IAL and LN-SUP. Prior to this Flugfelag Islands/Icelandair DC3s had visited Renfrew on regular passenger and freight charter flights in the late 1940s and 1950s.

In the winter schedules for 1958/59 BEA introduced another one of their fares initiatives: a cheap weekend return fare from Renfrew to Heathrow (as well as the Heathrow to Belfast and Edinburgh routes) set at £8 return for travel on a Saturday or Sunday, valid for a stay of up to eight days. This produced an almost immediate increase of 25 per cent at the weekends and by the end of the first year there was a massive increase of 50 per cent in weekend loads – and this despite the worst winter since 1948/49. Between November 1958 and February 1959 severe fog disrupted operations at Heathrow and Renfrew (as well as Birmingham and Manchester) on numerous occasions causing cancellations and diversions.

In February 1959 three different aircraft types visited for the first time, USAF Convair C-131D Samaritan (55–0291), BKS Airspeed Ambassador (G-ALZT), arrived on 10 February and a Curtis C46 (SE-CFA) of Transair Sweden the following day. Visits by Scandinavian airlines have always been a feature at Glasgow, Edinburgh and Aberdeen from the 1950s onwards. Apart from Transair Sweden, Scandinavian visitors to Renfrew in the 1950s and early 1960s included: Norronafly (Convair CV240), Fred Olsen (DC3, DC6, Viscount and Curtis C46), Braathens SAFE (DC3, DC4, DC6 and Fokker F27), Flying Enterprise (Canadair Argonaut and DC7), Finnair/AERO O/Y (DC3 and Convair CV440), SAS (Convair CV440 and DC6), Nordair A/S (DC6 – sub-charters for Loftleidir and Flufelag Islands), WIDEROE Flyveselskap (Nord 260, Nord 262), Kar-Air (Convair CV440 and DC6), Sterling Airways (DC6B), Ostermanair (DC7), Tor-Air (Curtis C-46 Commando) and Polaris Air Transport (DC3).

In addition to the Scandinavian, Irish and Icelandic flights further international flavour was added to the movements at Renfrew by Sabena and KLM. Sabena operated Convair CV440s to Ostend and Brussels. The first recorded visit of a CV440 was on 12 June 1959 when OO-SCO operated the Brussels service. KLM operated regular DC3 flights to and from Amsterdam.

BUA Vickers Viscount taxiing out to take off. (Ernie Brown)

Towards the end of the 1950s the sleek modern shape of the Vickers Viscount was now starting to replace the DC3 at Renfrew. For instance, in the second half of November 1958 there were seventy recorded Viscount movements against seventy-eight DC3 movements. Aer Lingus decided to replace the DC3 on their Dublin service with the F27 Fokker Friendship, with EI-AKA flying the first service on 11 December 1958.

In 1959 BEA started a Heathrow–Renfrew–Manchester–Heathrow freight service using aircraft leased from Dan Air. The period of the lease of the Dan Air aircraft was from 21 May 1959 to 31 December 1961. The first flight to Renfrew was undertaken on 25 May 1959 by Dan Air DC3 G-AMSS. The DC3 was replaced by the larger Avro York in 1960 which was also leased from Dan Air. Dan Air Yorks G-ANTI, G-ANTJ, G-ANTK and G-ANXN were used on this service as well as other BEA routes where the airline needed extra cargo capacity. The Avro York operated the service until BEA introduced their own Armstrong Whitworth Argosies on the route. It may be wondered why BEA had to charter aircraft from Dan Air to operate a new route, but the fact was that BEA did not have enough capacity at the time to use their own aircraft. The work on lengthening the runway at Birmingham during this period meant only Pionairs could be used while the work was carried out which entailed pulling the Pionairs in from other routes to operate Birmingham passenger schedules, thereby reducing the availability of the Pionair Leopards (Pionair Leopards were converted to carry cargo but were capable of quickly being converted back to passenger configuration). In addition to this BEA suffered a number of accidents in 1958/59 which further reduced capacity until new aircraft could be ordered to replace them. Finally, the introduction of the new Vickers Vanguard into service was delayed due to technical problems.

Towards the end of the 1950s, BEA realised that the Pionairs could not go on forever on the Scottish routes. However, the possibility of using the new Viscounts to replace them was dismissed as they would have provided overcapacity on some routes and a number of Scottish Airports were too small to handle the Viscount. Eventually BEA leased three Handley Page Dart Heralds (G-APWB, PWC and PWD) from the Ministry of Aviation for use on the Highlands and Islands routes. The Ministry of Supply had placed an order with Handley Page on 11 June 1959 for the three aircraft and leased them to the airline. The Heralds were ideal aircraft for use on the routes previously served by the Pionairs. The three Heralds were later sold to Autair on 1 November 1966.

The Military Side of Renfrew – Post-War and 1950s

Apart from the RAF, there were regular military flights into Renfrew by various other military air arms including the Royal Netherlands Air Force, with frequent visits by F27s, the USAF and USN (one example being 17108, a Douglas R4D-5 of the USN, in February 1959).

Like Abbotsinch, Renfrew became a transit point for aircraft returning to and coming from the USA. On 3 August 1948 13 F-80B Shooting Stars of the USAF 36 Fighter Wing arrived at Glasgow on the USAT *Barney Kirschbaum* with a further sixty-nine arriving on the USS *Sicily* on 7 August 1948. These F-80Bs were towed to Renfrew to continue their journey to Furstenfeldbrook AB in West Germany.

On 23 April 1953 twenty-four F-51 Mustangs in Arctic markings arrived from Prestwick with the crews returning to Prestwick in C-47A 42-24214. The Mustangs were cocooned for shipment by sea to the USA out of King George V Dock, Govan, two weeks later. In late 1953 thirty-nine USAF F-84E Thunderjets with serials in the range 49–2023 to 49–2121 arrived from Manston, Burtonwood and Charteroux on their way by sea to the Mobile AMA (Air Material Area) at Brookley AFB, Mobile Alabama. On 22 June 1953 eight L23A Beech Seminole communications aircraft were received at Renfrew from the carrier USS *Tripoli* for delivery to the US Army, with a further twelve arriving shortly afterwards.

Other regular military visitors were the RCAF (Royal Canadian Air Force) with their Bristol Freighters (with up to eight movements a month) from their base at Langar, near Nottingham, and then from Marville in France. There were also occasional visits from RCAF C-47s. These

602 Squadron DH Vampires shortly after delivery in 1951. (602 Museum)

RCAF Bristol 170 Serial 698. The canisters in the foreground contain Orenda engines for the RCAF Sabres undergoing maintenance. (Colin Lourie)

DH Vampires of 602 Squadron taking off with the familiar backdrop of Clydeside's cranes. (602 Museum)

RCAF Sabres behind the Lockheed hangars. (Douglas Rough Collection)

Two DH Vampires of 602 Squadron, WA179 and WA427, line up for take-off on Renfrew's main runway. (602 Squadron Museum)

602 Squadron DH Vampire parked in front of the original terminal at Renfrew. (Guy Henderson)

were support flights for the RCAF maintenance work carried out at the Scottish Aviation facility. Most of the RCAF Bristol Freighter and C-47 flights took place towards the end of the 1950s. The Bristol Freighter was a useful cargo aircraft at the time as it could transport a Sabre fighter complete with its wings removed and folded inside the interior.

On 13 November 1951 the Aircraft Carrier HMCS *Magnificent* docked at Pier 5 King George V Dock carrying thirty-five Sabre fighters of 410 and 441 Squadrons along with the air and ground crews for 410 Squadron. The Sabres were unloaded and transferred to Renfrew where they were serviced and flown to North Luffenham for their next three years of service. Scottish Aviation had established a facility at Renfrew in 1954 in addition to their main base at Prestwick. All the SAL subcontracted work at Renfrew (shipping/maintenance/assembly/cocooning) was controlled by 59 Air Depot Wing at Burtonwood. The Renfrew facility was also granted contracts to maintain aircraft for the RCAF and continued to do so up to 1960 before the work was transferred over to Prestwick. The RCAF aircraft maintained were Douglas C-47s, Beech Expeditors, Canadair CF-100s, Canadair Sabres and Canadair T-33s.

In 1957/58 the West German Air Force were given seventy-five ex-RCAF Sabre 5s as Canadian aid. Seventy-two of these Sabres were flown to Renfrew to be completely reworked by Scottish Aviation prior to delivery. The last of the Sabres were delivered to the WGAF in August 1958. Scottish Aviation held the contract to maintain and store the WGAF Sabre 5 and 6s at Renfrew and Prestwick.

The 1960s

BEA started 1960 by making available off-peak fares on the Heathrow–Renfrew route (as well as Belfast and Edinburgh). The off-peak fares were considerably cheaper than the standard fare but could only be used on late night and early morning flights. The cheaper fares had the desired effect and passenger numbers grew placing more strain on the facilities at Renfrew.

One exotic arrival on 31 July 1960 was N9812F, a Lockheed L749A Constellation. This elegant airliner was on a one-month lease from Miami Airlines to Loftleidir to operate the Reykjavik–Glasgow–Heathrow route.

The first visit of a not quite so exotic visitor was BEA Vickers Vanguard G-APEF which arrived at Renfrew on 20 December 1960, flying a round trip from Heathrow on its first commercial flight into Glasgow. After a hesitant start due to problems with its Rolls-Royce Tyne engines BEA Vanguards would come to dominate the Heathrow–Glasgow route along with the other main domestic trunk routes for the next decade. By the summer of 1961 BEA Vanguards were flying four return flights daily between Heathrow and Renfrew. On internal Scottish services Pionairs were gradually replaced as the three new Heralds took over, and Viscounts started to be used in place of the Pionairs on the Renfrew–Benbecula and Stornoway routes.

During this period BKS Air Transport made irregular flights to Glasgow. On 13 March 1962 they were taken to court by a group of minor creditors owed £24,000 by the airline. The

A FINNAIR Convair 440 Metropolitan and overview of the airport. (Ernie Brown)

Wideroe DC 3 LN–LMR. This aircraft was leased by Wideroe from May to September 1962 and was the first DC 3 in the fleet. Wideroe started operations in February 1934 and today is the largest regional airline in the Nordic countries. (Ernie Brown)

compulsory winding up order was opposed by a larger group of creditors owed £370,000 and the petition was dismissed. However, as a result of this court action BKS had to review its operations and a number of routes for which they had obtained licences from the ATLB, but not used, were dropped. One of these routes was Leeds–Glasgow which was considered to be unimportant to the BKS route network at the time.

In 1961 Lloyd International Airways was formed to provide air transport for the ships crews of the Mavroleon group of companies in the Far East, with a single Douglas DC4 G-ARLF. The airline had looked to expand their activities from this type of work, out of their Gatwick base, into other areas such as ad hoc charters and Ministry of Defence charter work. As part of Lloyd International's expansion the airline established a relationship with Mercury Holidays, a Glasgow tour operator. In the summer of 1963 Lloyd International flew holiday charter flights (or IT–Inclusive Tours as they were known) from Renfrew to Barcelona, Ostend, Palma, Perpignan, Rimini and Valencia in association with Mercury Holidays. The programme was mainly covered with one of the airline's DC4s, G-ARWK (G-ARLF having been destroyed in a refuelling accident at Malaga Airport on 8 October 1961), with back up during the busier periods provided by additional aircraft including a Douglas DC6 acquired from Alaska Airlines and registered G-ASTW.

Although the idea of package foreign holidays was still in its infancy in the early sixties, the flights operated by Lloyd International and Mercury proved to be popular, and equally popular destinations for Glasgow travellers at the time were Devon and Cornwall. Starways operated a Saturday service from Renfrew to Exeter Airport and onwards to St Mawgan (for Newquay). The first service was operated by Viscount G-ARIR for the summer holiday season from 3 June 1962 to 23 September 1962. The flight left Renfrew at 15.00 arriving at Exeter at 17.30 with a coach laid on from Exeter airport for the Torbay holiday resorts arriving at Torquay at 19.30. The service then flew on to Newquay from Exeter arriving at St Mawgan at 18.30 with the passengers arriving in Newquay itself at 19.00. The reverse service left Newquay and Torquay town terminals at 09.45 and 09.30 respectively, departing Exeter at 11.30 (having already departed St Mawgan at 10.30) and arriving at Renfrew at 14.00.

In March 1961 the airport general manager, Mr W.F. Murray, was forced to defend the cost of two temporary buildings which had attracted adverse press criticism. He explained

Flugdienst Convair 240 D-BEPE in May 1960. (Gordon Reid)

that the £15,000 cost of the two buildings was not a waste as they were to be transferred to Abbotsinch, and that without the buildings there would not be space to meet the numbers of passengers, which were growing at the rate of 20 to 25 per cent every year. He described the press comments as 'Tommy Rot'. The extensions were in addition to a prefabricated structure previously built in front of the terminal by the edge of the apron in 1959. The main problem was that many local people felt that the airport had outlived its usefulness and there had already been adverse press comment on 26 August 1960 when an article stated (after the announcement of Abbotsinch as the new airport) that there was no great sorrow from local people at its demise.

BEA started operating their Armstrong Whitworth Argosys on the Heathrow–Manchester–Glasgow route on 6 January 1962. The new Argosys were designed for pure freight carrying and enabled smoother handling of freight using pallets.

After the success of BEA's off-peak air fares in 1960 they offered up to 30 per cent midweek reductions on air fares within Scotland to try and iron out the weekend peaks. This new fare initiative was launched for the 1961 summer season.

By summer 1962 BEA's Vanguards were flying almost all the services between Heathrow and Renfrew and the use of the aircraft coupled with air fare marketing initiatives saw passenger

Grumman G73 Mallard G-ASCS owned by Ferranti. (Hugh Brown)

Douglas DC 4 D-ABEF of West German airline Continentale Deutsche Luftreederei on 1 May 1961. The airline was a charter carrier specialising in flights to Africa, the Middle East and the Far East. They went bankrupt in 1963. (Gordon Reid)

numbers grow by 21 per cent. The Vanguard had a large freight carrying capacity, as cargo also grew on the route by 20 per cent in its first full year of operation.

The introduction of the Handley Page Heralds on BEA's Highlands and Islands routes had been delayed by almost a year from the summer of 1961 when BEA had originally hoped to start using the aircraft. The first Herald G-APWB was leased to Jersey Airlines whilst G-APWC was used for the Duke of Edinburgh's lengthy Royal Tour of South America in 1962. G-APWB arrived in Renfrew on 10 March 1962 freshly painted in BEA colours after its lease to Jersey Airlines. G-APWD was delivered to Renfrew on 30 April 1962 and G-APWC arrived on 28 May 1962. The first commercial flight flown by a Herald was on 16 April 1962 when G-APWB flew from Renfrew to Sumburgh via Aberdeen, Wick and Orkney. With the arrival of the third and final Herald G-APWC, BEA finally withdrew the Pionair from service. By May 1962 there was only one route flown by the Pionair: Renfrew–Campbeltown–Islay. The final BEA Pionair service was flight number BE8679 on 19 May 1962 which departed Islay at 10.25 and arrived at Renfrew at 11.25 calling at Campbeltown on the way. The actual Pionair used was actually a Leopard (G-ALTT). Just before G-ALTT left Renfrew for the outbound sector to Islay all the BEA aircraft used on Scottish routes were lined up on the Renfrew apron for photographs. There was, in addition to G-ALTT, a Vanguard, Viscount, Herald and a Heron. For the summer 1962 schedule the Heralds covered three routes. The first Herald flew Renfrew–Campbeltown–Islay each morning except Sundays. It then flew Inverness–Wick–Orkney–Sumburgh, finally returning to Renfrew via Aberdeen. The second Herald left Renfrew at 09.40 daily, except Sunday, and flew the Aberdeen–Sumburgh route. It then flew Sumburgh–Orkney–Wick–Inverness–Renfrew. On Monday, Friday and Saturday the Herald flew an evening service Renfrew–Campbeltown–Islay–Renfrew. The third Herald flew Renfrew–Edinburgh–Aberdeen–Wick –Orkney and the return. The winter schedule was roughly the same but there was no evening service to Islay from Renfrew and the second service to Sumburgh flew on fewer days. An additional late evening service Renfrew–Aberdeen

Renfrew apron scene. All the BEA aircraft operating from Renfrew were brought together for this picture taken on 19 May 1962 to mark the retirement of the Dakota from the BEA fleet. (BA Museum and Archives)

was added with the Herald night-stopping at Aberdeen and returning to Renfrew the follow-ing morning

The first commercial jet airliner to land at Renfrew was a Sud Aviacion SE210 Caravelle EC-ARI of Iberia on 28 April 1962. The Caravelle was able to use the limited facilities at Renfrew but highlighted the fact that the larger jet aircraft coming into service in the late 1950s and early 60s would be unable to do so without severe payload restrictions. Iberia started a weekly summer service from Renfrew to Barcelona and Palma (some were routed through Manchester) with Lockheed Super Constellations on 1 June 1964. Most of the flights were operated by Super Constellation EC-AMQ. Prior to this Aviaco had operated a number of flights to Madrid with DC4 EC-APQ.

It had already been decided in November 1960 that the facilities at Renfrew were inade-quate to cope with larger aircraft and increased demand due to the fact that there was no room to expand. So, the then current facilities had to cope with demand until Abbotsinch was ready.

Over in the USA in 1961, Eastern Airlines had pioneered the concept of the 'Shuttle' service with an hourly hop between Washington DC, New York and Boston. This was a high fre-quency (every hour) walk on service where passengers were guaranteed a seat without any prior booking. The aircraft flew on time whether they were empty or full and it proved to be a great success for Eastern Airlines. BEA looked closely at the concept and announced in 1962 that they would introduce a similar service on two of their busiest routes: London to Paris and London to Glasgow. Their announcement gave a start date for the services to commence in September 1963 but the plan did not come to fruition. It is quite possible that BEA was starting to face competition from a number of independent airlines at the time and were attempting to look for ways to meet this competition. It was an innovative idea at the time but it would be many years before the 'Shuttle' idea actually came into being on the London to Glasgow route.

In 1962 Loganair, a name that would come to strongly feature in Scottish aviation, was founded at Turnhouse. The aviation division of Duncan Logan (Contractors) Ltd was formed

One of the two Renfrew-based BEA Herons undergoing a major overhaul in the BEA Engineering Hangar. (Colin Lourie)

on 1 February 1962 with Piper Aztec G-ARMH being delivered in June of that year to carry directors and staff between sites, and quickly expanded into air taxi and charter work. Duncan MacIntosh had set up an air taxi company called Capital Services (Aero) Ltd. Willie Logan was one of Capital's customers and had asked Duncan MacIntosh to be the pilot for their Aztec. Loganair then moved its base to Renfrew where it rapidly expanded.

One event that made the front page of the Scottish *Daily Express* on 12 June 1962 was the 'invasion' of Glasgow Airport the previous evening by triumphant Rangers fans returning from Russia via Copenhagen. The fans leapt over fences and obstacles and ran onto the apron celebrating the win. Fortunately there were no injuries.

A feature of the commercial aviation scene throughout the years has been the constant mergers or acquisition of various airlines. One example was Silver City, who were regular visitors to Renfrew with their DC3s and Bristol Freighters. They merged with Jersey Air Lines to form British United Airways (Channel Islands) and were known as BUA (CI) until their next reorganisation. Jersey Airlines had started a new service earlier that year on 2 June 1962 when Handley Page Herald G-APWE flew the first service from Renfrew to Jersey. Another well-known name lost to reorganisation was Starways which was absorbed into British Eagle at the end of 1963. The last service to be flown by Starways was DC3 G-AMSN which flew from Blackbushe into Renfrew and back again on 31 December 1963.

After the formation of the ATLB (Air Transport Licensing Board) in the spring of 1961 there was a rush of applications from the independent airlines to fly on routes served by BEA. The first serious competition to BEA on the trunk route Heathrow to Glasgow (as well as Edinburgh and Belfast) came from British Eagle. Harold Bamberg, the majority shareholder of British Eagle, had ambitious plans for the airline, and probably would have had considerably better success twenty or thirty years later, but in the early 1960s he faced the national airline BEA with virtually the full weight of the Government behind it. Bamberg changed the name of the airline back to British Eagle from Cunard Eagle in August 1963 (the airline's fourth name change, having originally started as Eagle Aviation Ltd in 1948), and on 3 November

OO-SCN Convair 440 Metropolitan and Icelandair Viscount TF-ISU, who formed the backbone of international scheduled operators, along with Aer Lingus and Loftleidir, from Renfrew, June 1960. (Gordon Reid)

1963 Bristol Britannia G-AOVT flew the first service between Heathrow and Renfrew with the first flights to Edinburgh and Belfast starting the following day (G-AOVT incidentally, was the first of fourteen Britannia 312s bought from BOAC by British Eagle, and is now preserved at Duxford).

Despite their request for greater frequencies, and to limit BEA's frequencies, the Air Transport Licensing Board granted British Eagle permission to operate only seven return flights a week on the Heathrow–Glasgow route without limiting BEA's capacity. British Eagle offered passengers trickle loading on the flights to London, a full meal service and seat selection on their Britannias (with sixteen first class seats and eighty-seven tourist class seats). BEA's response to the competition was to offer exactly the same facilities. Additionally, BEA also adjusted its schedules to mirror the British Eagle flights and increased capacity by 50 per cent. When asked to comment on their tactics, a BEA spokesman said:

> BEA have been expanding their routes and services for seventeen years to cater for the growing demand for air transport and we do not really need to borrow any ideas from Bamberg as to when and how to operate air services for the benefit of the traveling public.

Of course it can be argued that this was merely competition, but the odds were heavily stacked in BEA's favour. As will be seen later, British Airways (which BEA became when they merged with BOAC) was to react in a similar manner when British Midland started competing on the Heathrow–Abbotsinch route in the early 1980s. In addition, the route development costs to Glasgow and Edinburgh were in the region of £350,000, a substantial outlay for British Eagle. The airline unsuccessfully attempted to get increased frequencies which were necessary to justify their financial commitment but it was not forthcoming immediately. However, in 1964 British Eagle were allowed to increase their frequencies on the Glasgow-Heathrow route from seven to twelve round trips a week. This increased frequency started on 1 April 1964, still far short however, of the fifty-nine services a week operated by BEA.

Cambrian Airways had started a new Cardiff–Bristol–Glasgow summer service from 1 April 1962. Manchester and Liverpool were added to the route and the service would change between Manchester and Liverpool in later years and connections were provided by BEA from Glasgow to each of the northern airports during the winter schedules to connect with Cambrian flights to Cardiff and Bristol.

OO-CTH Douglas DC 6B of Sabena in February 1962. It was re-registered as OO-ABG with Belgian International Air Services, until she was written off in a landing accident at Milan on a cargo flight carrying 214 calves on 18 February 1966. (Gordon Reid)

The other serious challenge to BEA on the London route came from BUA (British United Airways). BUA had applied to the ATLB at the same time as British Eagle had applied to operate the Heathrow–Renfrew route. BUA were looking to fly to Renfrew from Gatwick rather than Heathrow but BEA had objected just the same as it had with British Eagle's application. However, BUA were granted a licence to operate the service on which they used their BAC1-11s. The first service did not start until 4 January 1966 with BAC1-11 G-ASJJ operating the first flight from Gatwick.

A new summer service was started by BEA to Palma in 1964, operating three days a week (Mondays, Wednesdays and Thursdays) via Manchester, using Vanguards.

A BEA Vanguard (G-APEE) suffered a collapsed nose wheel after a heavy landing on 6 November 1964. Just over a year later, on 27 October 1965, this same aircraft, coming from Turnhouse, crashed at Heathrow with the tragic loss of all on board.

The senior pilot on BEA's Herons was Captain David Barclay who had also been involved with the air ambulance service since its inception. Captain Barclay had been flying in Scotland since 1935. He joined BEA in 1947 and had flown 2,000 of the 5,500 air ambulance flights. His long and distinguished career came to an end on 30 April 1965 when he made his last scheduled flight on Heron G-ANXB from Renfrew to Barra via Tiree. The flight stewardess was his daughter who was working for BEA (the Herons did not normally carry stewardesses). Official and unofficial presentations were made at Tiree and Barra, including people who had been carried on the air ambulance service. It was the end of an era, and people like Captain David Barclay were its Scottish pioneers. His skill at flying in all kinds of weather helped to contribute to the safety record over the difficult and demanding terrain of the Highlands and Islands.

A shortlived route from Renfrew to Enniskillen (St Angelo) was started by British Midland Airways in 1964 using DC3s, but was stopped in 1965 having operated for just two summer seasons.

By 1965 BEA's Heralds were operating an intensive flying programme, especially during the peak summer months from 26 June to 4 September 1965. The Heralds also flew outside Scotland occasionally. In 1965 a Herald flew an evening Renfrew–Belfast–Renfrew service, taking fifty minutes each way.

Another route that took the Herald outside of Scotland was the Renfrew–Jersey service which operated once every fortnight during peak summer months. The journey took two hours and fifteen minutes each way with a forty-five-minute turnaround time in Jersey. What set this

BEA Armstrong Whitworth Argosy G-ASXM. BEAs Argosys took over from the leased Dan Air Yorks on the cargo service to Heathrow via Manchester. (John Martindale)

service apart from other Herald services was the fact that it was the longest sector and, despite being flown on a Sunday, it was the only Herald service which offered catering facilities.

The Heralds also flew air ambulance services from time to time when the Herons were unavailable. They also carried stretchers on scheduled flights as the wide door of the Heralds coupled with the low height of its rear door made it ideal for this type of work.

The Heralds were also ideal for cargo work and were used to take mail, newspapers and general cargo on the Scottish routes out of Glasgow. The one drawback of the aircraft was the fact that it was very costly to run and maintain, even with just three aircraft. BEA wanted to standardise its fleet as much as possible and decided to eventually replace the Heralds with Viscounts.

In 1965 BEA was keen to increase their cargo services and some of the Vanguard services from Heathrow to Renfrew were modified to operate in a mixed configuration where up to eight tons of freight was carried in the forward cabin and seventy-one passengers in the rear. There was concern about the pounding to the runway at Renfrew caused by the Vanguards. By 1965 it had been twelve years since any major work had been carried out on the main runway, and daily inspections of the runway were being carried out in the last years of service to check for cracking.

The major problem for Renfrew was the scale of overcrowding with growing passenger numbers. There was a great reluctance to spend any more money to improve the situation in what some described as a 'doomed airport'. Despite the worries over the inadequacy of the Renfrew facilities, Airport Director Ronald Read, at the end of 1965, stated that he felt the transit facilities at Abbotsinch would be inadequate. He quoted the passenger figures for 1964 which already exceeded that expected for 1965. Based on his concerns the airport committee made representations to the Ministry of Aviation to improve the facilities at no cost to the corporation.

The last scheduled departure from Renfrew was flown by BEA Vanguard G-APEN which left for Heathrow at 07.25 with the last airliner departure just over forty minutes later when Viscount G-APND of BUA left the runway at Renfrew for the last time.

Renfrew passed into history and the site has been built over, leaving just the odd reminder that a busy airport once existed there: part of the M8 follows the line of the former 08/26 runway, and on 23 October 1966 a cairn dedicated to the crew of G-AOFY who had lost their lives answering an air ambulance call in 1957 was unveiled by Captain David Barclay. The memorial is at the junction of Newmains and Sandy Roads.

2

ABBOTSINCH

The origin of the 700 acres known Abbot's Inch is uncertain but it is believed that the 'inch' was gifted around 1200 to Paisley Abbey by Walter Fitzallan, High Steward of Scotland. By the time of the establishment of the airfield in 1932 the spelling had become Abbotsinch.

The first occupants of the new airfield were 602 (City of Glasgow) Squadron who moved over from Renfrew on 20 January 1933 with their Westland Wapitis and remained for almost seven years. From May 1939 they were equipped with the Spitfire I/Ia. Following the United Kingdom declaring war on Germany on 3 September 1939, they detached a Flight to RAF Grangemouth on a daily basis as of 7 October 1939. A week later the whole squadron transferred to RAF Drem.

Two squadrons, 21 and 34, arrived from Bircham Newton within days of each other on 25 and 30 July 1936. Both squadrons operated Hawker Hind two-seat day bombers for inshore. They departed to Lympne on 3 November 1936.

No.269 Squadron moved to RAF Abbotsinch on 30 December 1936 for inshore patrol duties. W.E. Rankin (later Group Captain CBE, DSO) was the oldest officer in the squadron at the age of twenty-eight. Practically all the other officers and co-pilots were in their early twenties. The squadron consisted initially of one Flight of eight Avro Ansons 1s. The aircraft were not fully equipped and the crews only partly trained. Two further Flights of aircraft were added and they all had to be fitted with bomb racks, bomb sights, guns and radios, all drawn from RAF stores. As war drew closer a number of shipping firms in Glasgow were approached to enlist their co-operation in an ongoing programme to intercept inward bound ships and exchange lamp signals with them. This was valuable training for the squadron. In wartime interception of, and visual communications with, Royal Navy vessels was an important part of 269 Squadron's work, but in peacetime there was little opportunity to practice with RN vessels. On 17 January 1938 the squadron transferred to RAF Eastleigh in Hampshire before returning to Abbotsinch on 24 March 1938. All RAF Squadrons were ordered to their war stations at the end of September 1938, and 269 Squadron detached to RAF Thornaby, near Middlesborough on 29 September returning to Abbotsinch just over a week later on 6 October 1938. 269 Squadron spent the rest of 1938 and the first half of 1939 at Abbotsinch continuing to prepare for war. One tragedy which involved the squadron before the start of the war was the search for HMS *Thetis*. *Thetis* was a new T-class submarine which left Birkenhead for Liverpool Bay on 1 June 1939 to conduct her final diving trials. She disappeared. Ansons of 269 Squadron were sent from Abbotsinch to assist in the search. Sadly, *Thetis* had sunk with a loss of ninety-nine crew. She was later brought to the surface and re-entered service as HMS *Thunderbolt* before being sunk in the Mediterranean in 1943, giving her the unenviable accolade of being one the few military vessels to have been lost twice with all hands. One of the pilots of the 269 Squadron Ansons involved in the search for the *Thetis* was John Barraclough, later to become Air Chief Marshall Sir John Barraclough, who had joined Coastal Command in 1938.

On 26 July 1939 tragedy struck the squadron when fifteen Ansons in three formations of five were returning to Abbotsinch from Belfast. After crossing the Irish Sea they ran into bad weather over the Scottish hills. Anson K6255 crashed in heavy mist when its wing tip hit the

602 Hawker Harts at Abbotsinch in 1934. (602 Squadron Museum)

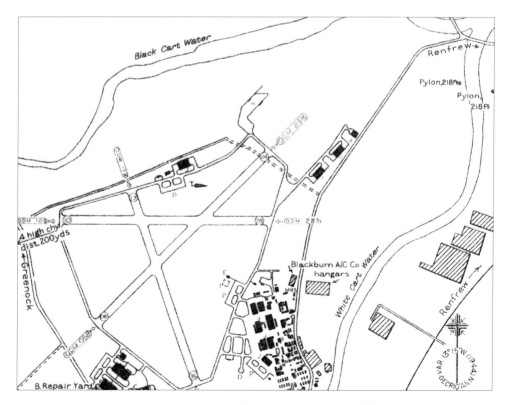

Abbotsinch layout after it became a Royal Naval Air Station. (Crown Copyright)

602 Squadron Hawker Harts in 1934 flying over RMS *Queen Mary* under construction at the John Brown Shipyard. (602 Squadron Museum)

top of Shield Hill, Inverkip, Renfrewshire. Sadly the pilot, Sergeant Robson, died later of his injuries. The squadron finally ended its association with Abbotsinch on 25 August 1939 when it was transferred to RAF Montrose.

Close to Abbotsinch the Blackburn factory at Dumbarton had started producing the Blackburn Botha I twin-engined torpedo and reconnaissance aircraft in 1939. Newly built Bothas were transported up the River Clyde to a slipway on the White Cart, a river which, in effect, formed the eastern boundary of the airfield. Here they were off-loaded to Blackburn's large, purpose-built hangar. Transportation was performed using a specially built lighter (at a cost of £4,135) named *Dumbrough* (an amalgamation of Dumbarton and Brough). The first Dumbarton-built Botha for the RAF was L6349 (actually the third production aircraft) which passed through Abbotsinch on 12 December 1939 on its way to 5MU at Kemble. The Botha was an unloved aircraft and was declared obsolete in 1943. By this stage there had been a number of crashes involving the aircraft, including two at Abbotsinch in 1940 (L6377 and L6390).

No. 2 Coastal Patrol Flight was formed on 9 October 1939 as a sub-unit of Coastal Command and was based at Abbotsinch until 27 May 1940. The unit flew de Havilland Tiger Moths and performed reconnaissance duties as well as being a deterrent to any U-boats by virtue of their mere presence.

418 Flight was formed at Abbotsinch in July 1940 with twelve pilots. They converted to (tropicalised) Hurricanes before departing on HMS *Argus* to Malta and RAF Luqa. There, along with the remaining Malta Defence Flight Gloster Sea Gladiators (of *Faith*, N5520, *Hope*, N5531, and *Charity*, N5519, fame), they reinforced the stretched, and very weak, air defences. On 2 August 1940 both Flights were reformed as 261 Squadron.

After the start of the Second World War four Polish squadrons were formed on British soil under the terms of the Agreement of Mutual Assistance that existed between Great Britain and Poland. The Air Ministry gave approval for the formation of a fifth squadron, No. 309 (Polish)

602 Squadron
Hawker Harts
flying over
Renfrew in 1935.
(602 Squadron
Museum)

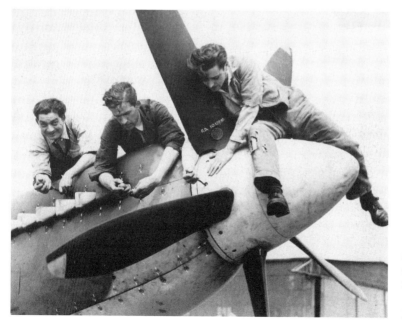

602 Squadron
members on a
Supermarine
Spitfire.
(602 Squadron
Museum)

Two Gloster Gladiators of 607 (County of Durham) Squadron RAuxAF at RAF Abbotsinch in the summer of 1939. (Robert Dixon)

607 Squadron – full squadron photograph at Abbotsinch, 1939. (Robert Dixon)

Army-Co-operation Unit. This unit of the Polish Air Force was formed on 8 October 1940 at RAF Abbotsinch. Within a fairly short period, on 6 November 1940, the unit was transferred over to RAF Renfrew.

Despite the fact that Abbotsinch was not commissioned as a Royal Naval Air Station until 1943, numerous Fleet Air Arm squadrons had started passing through, with the first being the Fairey Swordfish of 818 Squadron arriving from HMS *Furious* on 17 December 1939 and returning to the carrier just over a week later.

No.6 Aircraft Assembly Unit (AAU) was based at Abbotsinch from July 1940 until 1943 to assemble aircraft shipped into the Clyde docks from the USA. Additionally, Abbotsinch was used for the packing and dispatch of aircraft overseas, a function undertaken by No.3 Packed Aircraft Transit Pool. One example of their work was the packaging of Hawker Hurricanes which were sent out to Malta and West Africa on aircraft carriers.

Landplane version of the Vought-Sikorsky Kingfisher FN656 at Abbotsinch in April 1942. Most of the 100 supplied to the RN were the floatplane variant. (Phil Butler)

One of the most important units at the aerodrome was the Torpedo Training Unit (TTU) which was present from 19 March 1940 to 14 November 1942. The TTU moved from Gosport with its Fairey Swordfish and Blackburn Sharks, later taking delivery of Blackburn Bothas and Bristol Beauforts. The TTU had a dropping range off Troon, Ayrshire, which was the site of a number of accidents (some fatal) involving Swordfishes, Sharks and Beauforts.

A detachment of Bristol Blenheim IVs of 226 Squadron, used on Western Approaches patrols, arrived from Sydenham, Belfast, during May 1941, returning to Sydenham before the end of the month.

On 20 January 1942, 1441 Flight (correctly named 1441 Combined Operations Development Unit) was formed within 17 Group at RAF Abbotsinch on 20 January 1942. Elements of four squadrons attached to 1441 Flight took up residence for a short period. These were squadrons 239, 225, 18 and 21.

LAC Ernie Saunders, a member of 1441 Flight, remembered his time at Abbotsinch with fondness:

We were stationed at Abbotsinch for nearly a year and I regard it as one of the better places I visited. We were billeted in a Roman Catholic Convent on the Renfrew Road. It was quite unlike an RAF base as we lived a mainly alfresco existence with a complete absence of bull. We were issued with bicycles to go to and from the aerodrome and I can't recollect having a parade the whole time we were there. We used to call up the corner canteen on the way back from work and we were fed lovely fry ups by the local WVS (Woman's Voluntary Service) ladies. Then back to our billet to prepare for a few pints at the Station Bar, then the Templars dance hall filled with all the local lovelies. There were reputed to be nine females to every male in Paisley at that time. Bliss! I was only 18!

The Flight continued to operate at Abbotsinch until 19 October 1942 when 1441 Flight completed their move to RAF Dundonald (Bogside, Ayrshire) with six officers and ninety airmen.

In 1942 Grumman Martlets and Douglas Bostons had already started arriving by sea and were transferred by lighters from King George V Dock at Glasgow to the slipway on the White Cart at Abbotsinch as a part of the huge transatlantic operation to transfer war material from America that was getting underway. As the war progressed Lockheed P-38 Lightnings

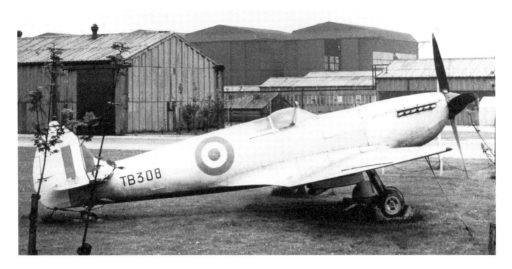

602 Squadron Spitfire LF XVIe TB308 on display at RAF Bishopbriggs, an RAF Balloon Station on the outskirts of Glasgow. Originally allotted to 602 in 1954 as an instructional airframe with the intention of being erected outside the new terminal at Renfrew Airport, it never came to pass and was scrapped at RAF Bicester in March 1961. (Guy Henderson)

and North American P-51 Mustangs started to appear in large numbers. There was a fairly wide variety of aircraft passing through in transit including, in May 1943, a group of two-seat reconnaisance Curtiss Seamews – another unloved aeroplane.

254 Squadron took up residence from 1 May to 1 October 1942 with Bristol Blenheim IVFs and Bristol Beaufighter VIs. Another unit based at Abbotsinch between 24 May 1943 and 6 March 1944 was 1680 (Western Isles) Communications Flight. Using various light communications aircraft, principally DH Dominies, the unit maintained contact with the remote airfields in the Hebrides. In September 1942 1680 Flight had acquired an impressed-into-military-service ex-civilian Fokker FXXII (HM159 ex-G-AFXR), but tragedy occurred on 3 July 1943 when the aircraft caught fire midflight and crashed into Loch Tarbert on the west side of Kintyre killing all twenty people on board including the Abbotsinch station commander, Wing Commander B.H. Jones.

A detachment of the Merchant Ship Fighter Unit was based at Abbotsinch from 23 May 1943 and was responsible for preparing 'Hurricat' fighters which were taken by barge via the White Cart to be installed on merchant vessels out to sea. These modified Hurricanes were placed on catapults on the ships to provide air cover for North Atlantic convoys.

On 11 August 1943 Abbotsinch ceased to be an RAF station and became a 'Stone Frigate'. RNAS Abbotsinch was commissioned as HMS *Sanderling* on 20 September 1943. At times up to 1,000 officers and ratings were stationed at Abbotsinch. Its main functions as an RN Air Station were as an aircraft maintenance yard and reserve aircraft storage space. An Aircraft Holding Unit (AHU) was established shortly after the RN took over.

It may be wondered why the RN should have taken over an RAF base at this stage of the war. However, there were a number of reasons: firstly, there was already an RAF base nearby at Renfrew; secondly, the RN needed an airfield close to the deep water anchorage in the Clyde to receive aircraft transported by sea under the Lend-Lease arrangements, and finally, the RN needed a transit refuelling and positioning base on the West Coast for 'work up' squadrons and aircraft as the bases on the East Coast of Scotland were that much more exposed to attack by German aircraft. There was a considerable amount of flying between Abbotsinch and RNAS Macrihanish, on the Kintyre Peninsula, involving aircraft 'working up'. In conclusion, Abbotsinch basically fitted RN requirements better than Renfrew. Renfrew, as previously mentioned, always suffered from a lack of space.

At Abbotsinch sometime between June and September 1953, this Fairey Firefly 5 VX434 '249/AC' of
Scottish Air Division 1830/1843 Squadrons RNVR. (Tom McFadyen)

There was a problem with Abbotsinch in that many felt the airfield was laid out over a
swamp! The whole airfield was in a waterlogged condition. There was always trouble with the
surface of the landing areas and the three initial runways were laid on embankments built to a
height of 4ft 6in above field level. American steel tracking was laid on top of this and drainage
was provided. Flying commenced the following year with 768 Squadron carrying out Deck
Landing Training (in Navy parlance, 'DLTs'), with carriers operating from the Clyde.

In 1943 No.1 (Scotland Air Training Corps) Gliding School was formed to train cadets in
the summer months of 1944 and 1945.

Amongst interesting aircraft to be seen at Abbotsinch in 1944 were two RN Grumman F7F
Tigercats (TT346 and TT349) on 8 December of that year. By the end of the war large numbers of Seafires and Sea Hurricanes were also passing through the airfield, in addition to US
military activity.

The largest number of helicopters to pass through in a single day (up to the closure in
1963) occurred on 17 January 1945. Nine of the former USA-based Royal Navy Flying
School (RNFS) Sikorsky Hoverfly Is (e.g. KK980) were being transported from Norfolk VA to
Glasgow docks on the aircraft carrier HMS *Thane* when she was torpedoed by U-1172. The
vessel was towed into Greenock and then Gare Loch where the helicopters were unloaded and
flown to the Receipt and Despatch Unit at Abbotsinch.

Abbotsinch Post-War

Although not as busy after the war, in terms of active squadrons, Abbotsinch continued its role
as an aircraft repair centre and storage facility. The airfield was later used for fitting and testing
new aircraft, inspecting and modernising them, in addition to the storage of old aircraft. In
1946/47 some surplus Seafires were removed from storage and given new leases of life with,
for example, the Aeronavale in France, or even the Irish Air Corps who received Seafire XV
PR302 in January 1947.

The post-war period saw large numbers of aircraft passing through to be returned to the
USA by sea. In addition to this, Abbotsinch became a dumping ground for aircraft from other

Sequence of pictures of Fairey Fireflies being transported from Abbotsinch to King George V Dock, Glasgow, to be loaded on HMS *Sydney*, during the Korean War. (Via Lee Howard)

Royal Naval air stations which were being run down after the war. Not all Lend-Lease aircraft were returned to the USA after the war as aircraft which were disposed of did not have to be accounted for. This is an over-simplification, but it meant that if, for example, the RN/RAF wanted to retain former Lend-Lease aircraft they would have to pay for them. The USA did not want vast numbers of redundant aircraft so many were simply dumped. An example of this was the departure from Greenock on 28 April 1946 of HMS *Chaser*, an escort carrier, with fifty-six aircraft on board. On 29 April the carrier had crossed the 100 fathom line (a 200m contour line, fifty nautical miles off the northwest coast of Donegal) and commenced ditching the aircraft into the sea. By 06.00 the following morning seventeen aircraft had been ditched, with the remainder being ditched by 12.26 that same day. The aircraft types are unconfirmed, but they were surplus to requirements and stored both at Abbotsinch and Renfrew.

The prototype Gloster Meteor F9/40 DG202 was flown to Abbotsinch by Glosters' chief test pilot, Squadron Leader Eric Greenwood, on 11 August 1945 and was transferred to HMS *Pretoria Castle*, moored in the Clyde, by lighter for engine running, taxiing and deck handling trials to test the suitability of jet aircraft for carrier work. This was the first jet aircraft to operate from a British aircraft carrier.

Aircraft in cocoons could regularly be seen at both Renfrew and Abbotsinch after the war. The process of embalming aircraft with preservative coats of Halothene (an Indian rubber solution) was first introduced in May 1947. This was the first time the process was used in the UK by any service.

1830 Squadron (commanded by Acting Lieutenant-Commander J.D. Murricane DSC RNVR) was formed on 15 August 1947, initially with three Seafire F.XVII, three Fairey Firefly Is and one North American Harvard two-seat trainer. 1830 was the first RNVR Squadron to be formed after the war. One of the little known activities of 1830 Squadron was the training of National Service pilots. On 8 January 1950 a Fairey Firefly FR1 (PP566) of 1830 Squadron flying from Abbotsinch crashed near the summit of Meikle Bin in the Campsie Fells, Stirling, with the tragic loss of both Lieutenant J. Arthur Robertson of Glasgow and Naval Airman J. Smith of Paisley. 1830 Squadron moved to Donibristle on 2 December 1950.

With the disbandment of the RVNR squadrons on 10 March 1957, the majority of surviving RN Grumman Avengers AS.4 and AS.5s congregated for storage at Abbotsinch before being passed on to France (forty-seven) in 1957/58 and Holland (twenty) in 1958 for use by their naval arms. This photograph, looking from west to east across the airfield, shows the stored Avengers and in the distance, stretching in a long line from from north to south, the mass of other stored types including Sea Hawks and Gannets, etc. (Douglas Rough)

Seahawk FAW6 XE399 in the Abbotsinch 'Air Day' static display. It is in the overall black finish used by the Airwork Fleet Requirements Unit (FRU) at Bournemouth Airport. Originally delivered to the RN on 13 June 1955 and sold for scrap at Fleetlands on 30 April 1967. (Colin Lourie)

First flight at Christchurch on 30 May 1959, and flown to AHU Abbotsinch on 10 June, DH Sea Vixen FAW.1 XJ514 was the first of many arriving there in preparation for operational use, modifications and storage prior to service issue. It appeared in the Static Display at the 1959 'Air Day' on 20 June before departing on 3 July for 892 Squadron at Yeovilton. (Douglas Rough)

The Scottish Air Division (SAD) RNVR was formed on 1 June 1952 at Donibristle. On 1 October 1952, 1830A Squadron was formed and shared 1830's aircraft. SAD, embracing both squadrons, returned to Abbotsinch on 1 November of that year. In March 1953, 1830A was re-numbered 1843 Squadron. From then until the disbandment of the RNVR squadrons on 10 March 1957, SAD remained at Abbotsinch swapping its Firefly AS.6s for Grumman Avenger AS.5s from November 1955.

The original runways were vastly improved by the laying of three tarmac and concrete runways, between 1950 and 1952, over what was then, following the Glasgow Blitz, a base of rubble. The runways were laid out in the familiar wartime triangular pattern.

The J.N. Connell Ltd Scrapyard at Coatbridge, Lanarkshire, in December 1961 – a sad ending for the Gannets, Sea Hawks and Avengers. (Gordon Reid)

Impetus was given to Abbotsinch with the start of the Korean War in 1950. This time the aircraft passing through Abbotsinch to board aircraft carriers bound for the Far East were Hawker Sea Furies, Grumman Avengers and Douglas Skyraiders. 602 Squadron, now equipped with DH Vampire FB.5s and Meteor T.7s, had moved over from Renfrew in June 1954 and remained there until they were disbanded on 10 March 1957. The RNVR Squadrons (1830 and 1843) were also disbanded along with the little-reported RAuxAF unit, 1967 Observation Post (AOP) Flight, parented by Perth (Scone Airfield) based 666 Squadron, which had been formed there on 1 May 1949. At disbandment 1967 Flight was equipped with Auster AOP.6s (e.g. TW578) and an Auster T.7, WE589.

As already mentioned, a feature of both Renfrew and Abbotsinch was their military links with the River Clyde and in particular with King George V Dock at Glasgow. After the war finished aircraft continued to come and go in both directions by sea.

By way of example, in April 1949 the Australian carrier HMAS *Sydney* picked up twenty-six Sea Fury FB.11s (including VW630) and twenty-seven Firefly FR.4/FR.5/AS.6 (including AS.5 VX372) for the Australian Navy, which transferred from Abbotsinch by road to the dock. The carrier arrived at Jervis Bay at the end of May 1949 and the Fireflies and Sea Furies were unloaded and taken to RANAS Nowra NSW by road.

HMAS *Sydney* repeated the same exercise in October 1950 when she picked up thirty-three Fireflies (including FR.5 WB371 and AS.6 WB510) and thirty-one Sea Furies (including FB.11 VX724) transferred from Abbotsinch. Again, the final destination in Australia was Jervis Bay, with the aircraft being transferred to RANAS Nowra by road.

602 Squadron – 'The End' – March 1957. (602 Squadron Museum)

Boulton Paul Sea Balliol T.21 WP325 used by the MTPS (and Station Flight) being towed into position for the Abbotsinch Air Day of July 1961. (Colin Lourie)

Line up of two unidentified Sea Hawks and five Sea Venom FAW.21s at the final Abbotsinch Air Day on 7 July 1962. Three of them are: ex-750 Squadron of RNAS Hal Far, Malta, and XG665 018/VL ex-Airwork of RNAS Yeovilton. They were all sold for scrap on 12 December 1962 to H.H. Bushell & Co., Birmingham. (Douglas Rough Collection)

Under the auspices of the Mutual Defense Assistance Pact (Act signed by President Truman on 6 October 1949) all bar one of 100 Grumman Avenger TBM-3Es arrived at Abbotsinch in 1953 via King George V Dock to fulfil the anti-submarine role. To plug the gap in AEW capability fifty AEW equipped Douglas Skyraider AEW.1s were also delivered to Abbotsinch by sea. Of these fifty AEW Skyraiders twenty were new aircraft diverted from USN production at El Segundo and the remaining thirty were refurbished aircraft from USN stocks. The first four of these Skyraiders (WT944, WT945, WT946 and WT947) arrived on board the USS *American Clipper* and were towed to Abbotsinch on 10 November 1951. These four aircraft went on to 778 Squadron Service Trials Unit (STU) at RNAS Culdrose later that month. The remaining forty-six aircraft were delivered via KGV during 1953, '55 and '56.

More aircraft went out to the Australian Navy in 1956 when HMAS *Melbourne* set sail on 11 March 1956 for Australia with sixty-five aircraft on board: thirty-nine DH Sea Venom FAW.53s (e.g. WZ893), twenty-two Fairey Gannet AS.1 and T.2 (e.g. T.2 XA514), one Meteor NF.11 (WM374), one Avro 707A (WD280) and two Bristol Sycamore HR.51 helicopters (e.g. XL502).

Other air arms were also involved in taking aircraft from storage at Abbotsinch. Fifteen ex-RN Harvards, which had originally been in storage at Arbroath, were delivered to the Portuguese Air Force between January and March 1956 following refurbishment at Abbotsinch. Their serials were FT965, FT966, EZ403, FT971, EX976 and the remainder fell in the range EZ281 to EZ438. They were given Portuguese Air Force serials 1655 running consecutively through to 1669 for the fifteen aircraft.

Twenty Grumman Avengers went to the Netherlands in early 1958. France's Aeronavale also took delivery of twenty-seven Avenger AS4s in 1957 (e.g. XB296) followed by a second batch of twenty Avenger AS5s the following year. Part of the first batch of Aeronavale Avengers embarked on board the French aircraft carrier *Dixmude* on 15 July 1957 for Toulon. The ex-RN Avengers still carried their British serials (e.g. XB296). The second batch of twenty Avenger AS.5s (e.g. XB404) also departed on the *Dixmude* for Cherbourg on 21 March 1958.

The closure of RNAS Anthorn and RNAS Stretton in 1958 and Donibristle in 1959 brought more aircraft to Abbotsinch for storage including Supermarine Attackers (mostly ex-RNVR) were initially stored in the former Blackburn hangar and latterly on the airfield prior to scrapping.

The last operational version of the Grumman Avenger in Royal Navy service was the Electronic Counter Measures (ECM.6/6B) variant. Seen here in July 1961, they were among the last aircraft to be disposed of from Abbotsinch in 1963 prior to its closure. One ECM.6B, XB446, was saved from the smelter and is now in the Fleet Air Arm Museum at RNAS Yeovilton, Somerset. (Douglas Rough Collection)

Cocooned in 'Halothene' (an India rubber solution) and powered by an Armstrong Siddeley Double Concrete engine, AS.1 WN449 was sold for scrap on 20 June 1963 to J.N. Connell Ltd in Coatbridge, Lanarkshire. It was one of many aircraft from the air station which ended their days there just prior to the closure of RNAS Abbotsinch. (Douglas Rough Collection)

WJ231, a Hawker Sea Fury FB.11 of Airwork FRU, Hurn, taxiing to its position in the static display for the 8 July 1961 'Air Day', followed by a Supermarine Scimitar F.1 XD212 '614' of 736 Squadron, RNAS Lossiemouth. Crowd control, or Health and Safety, was obviously not as much of an issue in those days as it is now. (Colin Lourie)

Supermarine Attacker coming in to land. This jet aircraft was unusual because it had a tail wheel rather than a nose wheel, which was due to the original design being for the propeller-driven Supermarine Spiteful. (Guy Henderson)

By November 1960 the Skyraider AEW.1 was replaced in RN service by the AEW3 Gannet. Between December 1961 and May 1962 ten of the Skyraider AEW.1s which were stored at Abbotsinch were transferred to Prestwick by road to be refurbished and modified by Scottish Aviation Ltd for delivery to Sweden. The aircraft had been bought as part of a batch of twelve by the Swedish company Svensk Flygtjanst AB. This was a private company which operated target tugs under contract to the Flygvapnet, which was to become the intended use of the reworked Skyraiders which were given civilian Swedish registrations.

The first 'Air Day' was held in 1957 and was very popular with the public, continuing on an annual basis until 1962.

The first two Sea Vixen FAW1s arrived on 10 June 1959 (XJ514) and 11 June 1959 (XJ513) direct from the production line in Christchurch. XJ513 appeared in the static display at the Abbotsinch open day on 20 June 1959. Abbotsinch was the nominated unit for preparing the Sea Vixen FAW1s in their operational roles before departing to their squadrons and were a regular feature of the airfield's movements in its final years as a naval station. Fairey Gannets had started to arrive at the AHU (Aircraft Holding Unit) for disposal from 1958 to 1960, then, between 1960 and 1963, they were sent to scrapyards around the country to be broken up. These included types AS1, AS4, T2 and T5. In the early 1960s a number of Gannets could be seen awaiting disposal in the scrap yard of J.N. Connell Ltd in Coatbridge, Lanarkshire. Some of the stored ex-RN Gannets were refurbished by Fairey Aviation and sold to Indonesia. One example was Gannet AS1 WN394 which became Indonesian Navy AS-09.

The last aircraft to leave Abbotsinch before it finally closed on, of all days, Friday 13 September 1963 were:

12.47 Gannet AS.1 XA363 to RNAS Culdrose (flown by Metcalfe)
14.23 Whirlwind to RAF Leuchars (flown by Beggs)
14.25 Sea Prince T.1 WF131 to Rochester (flown by Richardson)
14.40 Sea Vixen FAW.1 XJ605 to RNAS Brawdy (flown by Lawson)

The pilot, named Metcalfe, had flown the second last Sea Vixen (XJ570) out the previous day to Yeovilton and had been brought back by the Sea Prince (which belonged to the Shorts Ferry Pool at Rochester) to fly the Gannet (which had been used by the Maintenance Test Pilots School at Abbotsinch) to the School of Aircraft Handling at Culdrose. 663 Volunteer Gliding School, which had been resident at Abbotsinch since March 1960, also disbanded in September 1963. It operated Slingsby products, namely the Sedbergh TX.1 (e.g. XN186), Cadet TX.3 (e.g. XN252) and Prefect TX.1 (e.g. WE983).

HMS *Sanderling* was finally decommissioned on 31 October 1963. The station's crest and bell were handed over by the station's last commanding officer, Commander John Mannering RN, to a representative of the Ministry of Civil Aviation, and was displayed in the Sanderling Bar within the airport's new terminal building

After the official closure the accommodation blocks were used for a short period to house personnel from the Royal Navy bases at Faslane and Rosyth.

The New Glasgow Airport

An announcement was made by the Minister of Aviation, Peter Thorneycroft, on 14 November 1960 that Abbotsinch Royal Naval Air Station would be developed to take the place of Renfrew. Following the decision by the Government in 1961 that major airports should be decentralised from the State and run by the municipalities they served, Glasgow Corporation decided on 27 June 1963 that it would take over the running of the new airport at Abbotsinch once it had been developed as Glasgow's new airport. They agreed that they would pay £2.5 million of the £4.3 million needed to develop the airport. They also agreed to pay £250,000 for the purchase of the airfield site plus a further £80,000 for equipment to be transferred from

BEA Viscounts G-AOHW & G-APKF, 13 June 1967. (John Martindale)

BEA Vickers Vanguard G-APEC, 28 August 1967. G-APEC crashed at Aarsele, Belgium, on 2 October 1971, flying from Heathrow to Salzburg, with the loss of eight crew and fifty-five passengers. (John Martindale)

Renfrew Airport. Safeguards against losses of over £100,000 for the first seven years of operation were also agreed.

The new terminal building was designed by Sir Basil Spence, Glover and Ferguson, with John Laing Construction acting as the main contractors. BEA invested £1 million in new facilities (including the new engineering base) at Abbotsinch and had some input into the design of the terminal building by suggesting the airport's unusual pre-flight passenger handling system which was later copied, in some respects, in Heathrow's Terminal One. There had been a proposal to dismantle the terminal at Renfrew and re-erect it at Abbotsinch but the idea was dropped when it was clear that a new and much larger terminal was required. The engineering

British Eagle Vickers Viscount 755 G-AOCC on 16 June 1967. It was sold to Invicta Airways in February 1968 and withdrawn from use in August 1969 at East Midlands Airport. (John Martindale)

facility was not ready for operations until 5 October 1966. There had been hopes that the new airport would have been ready by 1964. A newspaper article on 16 November 1961 expressed doubts that the airport would not open until 1965 until the Royal Navy moved its Sea Vixens which were still being maintained there to RNAS Brawdy in Wales.

The first aircraft to land was actually by mistake. On 26 April 1966, RAF Percival Pembroke WV703 had intended to land at Renfrew but came down on the Abbotsinch runway in error. The new airport officially opened for business on 2 May 1966, formally opened by HM the Queen the following month on 27 June. Glasgow's new airport had two runways, 06/24 at 6,720ft long and a secondary runway 10/28 at 3,570ft long. The new terminal had two aircraft piers, or 'fingers', for aircraft parking. This new design was incorporated in the new terminal buildings at Gatwick and Manchester. The terminal itself was spacious, bright and modern looking. A considerable effort had gone into giving the city a first class airport, and it compared favourably with other UK and continental airports of a similar size.

On 1 May 1966, the day before the official opening, there were three BEA movements: Herald G-APWB, Heron G-ANXB and Viscount G-AOYO, along with the arrival of a few light aircraft. There were a number of 'first visits' after Abbotsinch opened for business. On 2 May 1966 the following aircraft arrived: G-APEI, the first Vanguard (BEA), positioned from Renfrew at 02.04, departing at 08.04 for Heathrow; G-ARJN Comet (BEA) was the first jet to visit of this type; G-AOVE was the first Britannia (British Eagle); G-ASJC the first BAC1-11 (BUA); EI-AKA Fokker Friendship F27 (Aer Lingus) the first visit by a non-UK registered aircraft and the first of its type to visit. The first Comet to land (BEA's G-ARJN) was the first of a new twice-daily service from Heathrow (departing Heathrow at 07.30 and 17.30) which was intended to help meet growing competition on the London route from BUA with BAC1-11s to Gatwick and British Eagle who were in the process of introducing the BAC1-11 on their Heathrow service. A proving flight had been made by British Eagle BAC1-11 G-ATTP on 2 May 1966. However, despite the Comet shaving fifteen minutes off the Vanguards' flying time the congestion at Heathrow often wiped out this advantage.

Whilst Edinburgh's Turnhouse could be said to be the Scottish terminus for rugby charter flights then Glasgow could be said to be the Scottish terminus for football charter flights (although there were occasional rugby connected flights to Glasgow just as Edinburgh received

Britannia Airways Bristol Britannia G-ANBA, 27 July 1968. (John Martindale)

flights connected to football). The first aircraft to visit Abbotsinch in connection with football was Condor Flugdienst's Viscount D-ANOL which arrived from Frankfurt on 5 May 1966 for the Borussia Dortmund match against Liverpool at Hampden Park that day for the final of the UEFA Winners Cup. For those that are interested, Borussia Dortmund won 2-1 after extra time. Liverpool was managed at the time by the legendary Scot Bill Shankly. Nevertheless, this was the first of many football charter flights into the airport. Also on 5 May 1966 two Loftleidir aircraft passed through; DC6 TF-LLC from Keflavik to Amsterdam and CL44 (the first visit of a CL44) TF-LLF operated in the reverse direction to TF-LLC.

Two services started before the end of the first month's operations. The first was a weekly summer service by the Yugoslavian airline Adria Airways, which was to Ljubljana via Manchester, with the initial flight being undertaken by Douglas DC6 YU-AFE on 21 May 1966. Within a week, on 24 May, Autair started their new service to Blackpool with Ambassador G-ALZS undertaking the first flight. Autair also introduced Hs748s on the route to Blackpool, with G-ATMJ being the first of its type to visit on 31 May.

Invicta Airlines based at Manston were irregular visitors, flying mainly to and from Rotterdam (flying Bulbfields charters) in DC4s. Viking G-AHOW was also used on occasions. Autair was also involved in these Bulbfields charter flights with DC4 G-ASZT operating a Rotterdam charter on 16 May 1967.

On 10 May 1966 Britten Norman Islander G-ATCT flew up to Abbotsinch from the Britten Norman factory at Bembridge on the Isle of Wight to demonstrate its short take-off and landing capabilities to Loganair. The company was impressed with the aircraft, and despite a competing offer from a Dornier Do28 Skyservant, Loganair ordered two Islanders for use on inter-island services in the Northern Isles. Prior to the first of those arriving company demonstrator G-ATWU was used in the summer of 1967 before Loganair's first two aircraft arrived in August, registered G-AVKC and G-AVRA.

The first emergency was handled before the first month of operations was finished when N246, a Convair 240 of the FAA (US Federal Aviation Administration) made an emergency landing on 29 May 1966.

Aer Lingus and Aer Turas operated a variety of types into Abbotsinch including Bristol 170s and ATL-98 Carvairs on freight services, Viscount 800 series and the BAC 1-11s, with EI-ANG being the first Aer Lingus BAC1-11 visitor on 18 May 1966. Aer Lingus also leased Douglas DC7s PH-DSC, PH-MAK and PH-DSL of Dutch Charter operator Martinair which operated a number of flights from Dublin to Abbotsinch in 1966.

Air Ulster DC 3 G-AMJU on 13 June 1968, with USAF Convair VC-131A 0-25798 of 7101st ABW (Air Base Wing), Wiesbaden (West Germany), parked at the end of the pier. (John Martindale)

Lufthansa Boeing 707 D-ABUJ on 16 April 1969; one of nineteen aircraft bringing in West German football fans that day. (John Martindale)

The Italian charter airline SAM (Societa Aerea Mediterranea) flew their DC6s on holiday charters to Venice and Pisa for the summer season in 1966. Another charter operator which would be frequently seen at Abbotsinch in years to come was the Spanish airline Aviaco which made their first visit to the airport on 27 May 1966 with DC4 (EC-AEK) operating a charter flight to Madrid.

One airline which had a strong Scottish identity was Caledonian Airways. However, their main base was at Gatwick and they operated their Scottish flights mainly from Prestwick as opposed to Glasgow. The first Caledonian aircraft to visit Abbotsinch was Bristol Britannia 300 G-AOVI on 21 May 1966. Part of the reason for Caledonian using Prestwick was that they flew a large number of transatlantic flights which required use of Prestwick's better facilities and, as will be discussed later, because of Government directives.

On 3 July 1966 Air France started a new Paris service with F-BKGZ which was the first visit of a Caravelle. Air France also visited with Caravelle F-BJTN on 17 July 1966 which operated a flight to and from Nice.

BUA had been operating the Gatwick route with BAC1-11s in competition with BEA's Comets (to Heathrow) on the London route. However, on 2 July 1966 two flights to and from Gatwick were flown with VC10 G-ASIX. This was the first visit of this graceful airliner which substituted for the normal BAC1-11. This was followed just over a week later, on 10 July 1966, by BUA VC10 G-ATDJ and again on 16 July by G-ASIW. These three VC10s represented BUA's VC10 fleet.

If an aircraft and airline could be said to represent an era at an airport then the late '60s to the early '80s at Glasgow could be said to be symbolised by the BEA Trident. The first Trident to land was G-ARPD on 3 July 1966 on a proving flight to and from Heathrow. BEA was introducing the Trident on its prestige routes and had always viewed London–Glasgow as its premier domestic route. Another BAC1-11 operator was British Eagle. G-ATPL was used for the first time (on a scheduled flight) on the Heathrow service on 27 July 1966.

One unusual event occurred on 18 August 1966 which was the diversions of three aircraft (G-ASYF the ACE Scotland Constellation plus two Caledonian Britannias) to Abbotsinch from Prestwick because of fog! Prestwick was generally regarded as the diversion airport when most other UK airports were fogbound. Indeed, there were occasions during this period and during the 1950s when Prestwick was one of the very few northern European airports open when nearly all the others were fogbound.

During its first three months of operations Glasgow handled over 400,000 passengers and 17,000 aircraft movements. August 1966 saw a most unusual sight for a civil airport when no less than eight US Navy Lockheed P-3 Orions passed through on 11 August and again on 20 August when the same eight Orions made their way from the Azores to Norway.

ACE Scotland (Aviation Charter Enterprises) was formed in January 1966 as a subsidiary of ACE Freighters (formed at Gatwick in March 1964) to operate tours from Glasgow to the Mediterranean with Lockheed Constellation G-ASYF. The aircraft was given an overhaul by Scottish Aviation at Prestwick and undertook its first commercial service to Barcelona and

Donaldson International Bristol Britannia 312 G-AOVC on 7 June 1969. This aircraft inaugurated the first regular transatlantic service by a British turboprop aircraft on 19 December 1957, operating for BOAC. (John Martindale)

Palma on 16 July 1966. There were also flights to Athens, Rome and Rimini. It was a shortlived operation, however, with its last commercial flight taking place on 10 September 1966, and the airline ceased operations on 14 September 1966.

Emerald Airways started a new service on 16 September 1966 to Londonderry (Eglinton) and Belfast with leased DH Heron G-ALZL. The Heron was replaced by Short Skyvan G-ATPF on the service a week later. The service started as six days a week before it became weekly, and in the peak summer season of 1967 the Skyvan operated a thrice-daily schedule. A DC3 EI-APJ was added on 10 December 1966 to operate two services a week. After the demise of Emerald Airways, Air Ulster took over their routes and operated a Glasgow–Londonderry (RAF Ballykelly) service from December 1967 with ex-BUA DC3s. The airline ceased operations on 6 January 1970.

By October 1966 the runway work required to bring Islay, Sumburgh and Orkney up to a standard suitable enough to accommodate Viscounts was completed. BEA then withdrew the Heralds from service. The end of BEA Herald operations in Scotland officially came to an end on 31 October 1966 when Herald G-APWB flew Islay–Campbeltown–Abbotsinch (the same route as the last Scottish Pionair flight). The aircraft was commanded by Captain Burnett and left Islay as BE8679 at 11.30, arriving in Campbeltown at 24.45. It left Campbeltown carrying thirty-four passengers at 24.05 and after a low pass over the airfield went on to Abbotsinch arriving there thirty minutes later. The three Heralds (G-APWB, G-APWC and G-APWD) were returned to the Ministry of Aviation who sold them on to Autair on 1 November 1966.

Autair International Airways started a Glasgow-Blackpool-Luton return service (on Tuesdays, Wednesdays, Thursdays and Saturdays) shortly after the opening of Abbotsinch using their Ambassadors initially but replacing them with Heralds and then Hs748s.

By the end of its first year Abbotsinch had handled 34,397 aircraft movements and 1,291,388 passengers. The millionth passenger since Abbotsinch was opened in May was handled on 20 December 1966.

By January 1967 BEA Comets were flying twice daily on the Heathrow route for several months, and despite the competition from BUA on the Gatwick/London route and attempts by British Eagle to increase their frequencies, BEA more than held their own. Occasionally BEA Tridents would fly the Heathrow service during this period, for example Tridents G-ARPI and G-ARPL were used on 9 January 1967. Tridents officially started on the Heathrow

KLM Douglas DC 9 PH-DNN, loading cargo, 27 March 1970. (John Martindale)

route (replacing the Comets) on 3 April 1967 with G-ARPT flying the first service. BEA had two unfortunate incidents at Abbotsinch in early 1967:Viscount G-AOJC made an emergency landing with undercarriage problems on 27 January, and the following month part of the undercarriage fell off Vanguard G-APED shortly after landing.

In addition to the occasional diversion from Prestwick, as previously mentioned, Abbotsinch also acted as a diversionary airport for other airports. This was particularly the case with Edinburgh. The main runway at Turnhouse was badly aligned which resulted in numerous diversions over the years due to crosswinds. The problem continued until the opening of the new runway at Turnhouse in 1977. For instance, there were seven airliner diversions from Turnhouse to Abbotsinch on 27/28 February 1967. The following month also saw diversions to Abbotsinch by three Loftleidir CL44s which had been diverted from Keflavik.

In June 1967 a suggestion was put forward by twenty-five British and foreign airlines that Prestwick and Abbotsinch be renamed 'Glasgow McIntyre' and 'Glasgow Meldrum' respectively, named after Prestwick aviation pioneer David McIntyre and the late Sir James Meldrum, former Lord Provost of Glasgow. Both men had been closely involved with the development of the respective airports. However, Glasgow Corporation refused to consider the proposal, although in Prestwick's case the BAA were more amenable to a name change – though they did not want the name 'Glasgow' to be included. However, the proposed name changes came to nothing.

BUA started an Ostend service with Viscount G-APTC operating the first flight on 7 May 1967. BEA operated a weekly Glasgow–Palma service between May 27 and October 14 using Vanguards. This was in addition to the twice weekly Glasgow–Manchester–Palma BEA service. There were some alterations to BEA schedules. The Glasgow–Inverness Viscount service was routed via Edinburgh and the Glasgow–Aberdeen night service was extended to Wick for three nights of the week. Neither of these two changes generated much additional traffic and both the extensions to both Wick and Edinburgh were dropped in September 1968.

Probably the first large use of aircraft charters for a football match took place between 24 and 26 May 1967 when thirty-five aircraft (from thirteen airlines) were used to transport Celtic fans to Lisbon. Celtic themselves travelled to Lisbon in Dan Air Comet G-APDO on 23 May (coincidentally the first visit of a Dan Air Comet to Abbotsinch) and returned in

Loganair Beech 18 G-ASUG, 1970, now beautifully preserved at the Museum of Flight, East Fortune. (Charlie Stewart)

another Dan Air Comet G-APDK on 26 May. The following weekend saw another series of football-related charters (only eighteen aircraft this time) to Nuremberg.

Although Iberia had operated a Caravelle into Renfrew and Spanish charter airlines had already been flying from Abbotsinch, the first visit by Iberia was not until 31 May 1967 when Caravelle EC-ARL flew a service to Palma.

Although charter aircraft would substitute scheduled airline work and other charter airline work, an unusual substitution took place on 2 June 1967 when DC6 YU-AFB flew the Adria Airways charter flight to Ljubljana. Although it was carrying the civil registration YU-AFB, this DC6 was actually operated by the Yugoslav Air Force under serial No.7452 since its transfer from the national airline JAT in 1966. YU-AFB was later transferred again to Adria Airways in 1970/71 to operate charters.

The first Loganair Islander service was to Oban and Mull on 1 September 1967 with G-AVRA operating the service. Later that year a Beech C-45H arrived from Prestwick for Loganair on 25 November 1967. This was registered N15332 (an ex-Royal Canadian Air Force model, serial No.1533) and was reduced to spares for the Loganair Beech 18 G-ASUG which arrived from Leeds on 25 May 1968.

BMA started a new Leeds/Bradford–Edinburgh–Glasgow service with Viscount G-AVKA on 3 October 1967. There was a rail strike in October 1967 which saw eight different aircraft from five different British airlines flying in newspapers to Abbotsinch on 22 October.

An unfortunate accident occurred on 18 July 1967 when Viscount G-AOYO was crew training for Cyprus Airways. The Viscount had made a number of 'touch and go' landings when it overran the runway and was severely damaged. The aircraft was dismantled and taken by road to Marshalls of Cambridge for repair. G-AOYO was eventually put back into service in May 1968.

Ironically, considering BEA was the national domestic and European airline and the Trident was to be a main feature at Abbotsinch in years to come, the American tri-jet competitor of the Trident, the Boeing 727, visited Abbotsinch as frequently as the Trident in the immediate years after the opening of the airport. At the time there was a lot of debate amongst airlines about the key attributes of new aircraft, and the Boeing 727 and HS Trident were marketed head-to-head. However, BEA's history of interfering in aircraft design, together with UK manufacturers' unwillingness to meet the national airline's design requirements, resulted in an aircraft with limited international appeal. The Trident was advanced for its day having been developed with the ability to land 'blind' at airports such as Glasgow and Heathrow where fog could be a problem. In the end only 117 Tridents were built, more than half for BEA, and the aircraft was seen much more at Glasgow than the more ubiquitous (in world terms) 727.

Regular 727s included TF-FIE and TF-FIA of Icelandair, CF-FUN of Wardair and N7271 of Braniff International. N7271 had landed on a diversion from Keflavik in Iceland on 4 February 1968 four months before the first visit of a Trident 2 (G-AVFD) which arrived on 2 June 1968. The Trident 2 was less common at Glasgow due to the fact that BEA used it on the longer continental sectors, although it appeared reasonably regularly throughout the '70s at Glasgow.

BUA started a new service to Amsterdam via Newcastle on 2 April 1968 with the first flight undertaken by BAC1-11 G-ASJI. This aircraft type was destined to be seen at Glasgow for over thirty years in regular service. Another new service which started only a few days later than the BUA service was Air Ulster. Their new Belfast service got off to an unfortunate start on 8 April 1968 when DC3 G-AMWV arrived on the first flight from Belfast and the aircraft had to be withdrawn from service because of a technical fault.

On 1 April 1968 BEA introduced Tridents on the Glasgow–Birmingham–Paris route. Another first visit of type on 8 May 1968 was a DC8 (PH-DCD) of Martinair which arrived from Luxembourg and went on to Amsterdam. The following day, 9 May 1968, a small but not insignificant aircraft landed and took off for Santa Paula in California via Stornoway, the Faroes, Iceland, Greenland, across Canada and the USA. The pilot had to wait for five days for a break in the bad weather to continue his journey from West Germany. Little more than a powered glider with a 36hp VW engine, the Fournier RF4D, registered N1700 and named the *Spirit of Santa Paula*, was piloted by Mira Slovak, a Continental Airlines captain who had arrived in the USA from Czechoslovakia as a penniless immigrant. He flew the tiny aircraft all the way to California but crashed on approach to his final destination of Santa Paula. Mira Slovak survived the crash and the aircraft was repaired and now hangs in the Museum of Flight in Seattle.

Wardair Canada were passing through the airport on regular charters, but at the end of 1967 announced that in 1968 all their operations would be transferred to Prestwick, partly due to Government pressure to use Prestwick for all transatlantic operations and partly due to larger Boeing 707s being introduced, which were better suited to Prestwick with its longer runway. Despite this announcement the first visit to Glasgow by a Boeing 707 proved to be CF-FAN of Wardair which arrived on 23 July 1968 (although Boeing 707s G-AVZZ and G-AWDG of British Eagle had performed overshoots earlier that year in April). The 6,720ft runway at Glasgow was marginal in certain meteorological conditions if a 707 was fully loaded and heading across the Atlantic.

BEA's Herons had more or less flown the same schedule since the loss of G-AOFY in September 1957. They had their schedules altered to include a summer service from Glasgow to Barra flown seven days a week, making Barra the first Scottish island to have a Sunday service. The other conservative Scottish islands had long resisted Sunday services and continued to do so. Tiree was served by a six-days-a-week schedule from Glasgow with an additional evening service for three days of the week. Icelandair started a new summer service with Fokker F27 TF-FIL flying in from the Faroe Islands on 25 May 1968.

After the rail strike of October 1967 another rail strike in June 1968 saw a similar number of aircraft fly in to Abbotsinch on newspaper flights on 30 June (eight aircraft from five airlines) and 7 July (nine aircraft from six airlines).

One unusual visitor on 13 July 1968 was an IL18 HA-MOI of MALEV, the Hungarian airline, which arrived from and departed to Budapest. This was the first visit of a Russian built aircraft.

A significant boost to cargo services at the airport came with the start of a new dedicated five times a week freighter cargo service by KLM to Amsterdam via Manchester. The first flight was on 2 September 1968 with freighter DC9-32 PH-DNO. It has always been the case that freight from Scotland was generally sent via road to England or carried in mixed freight/passenger configuration aircraft because there was rarely enough to justify full cargo loads, particularly on a scheduled cargo service. With the exception of the scheduled BEA cargo service started at the end of the 1950s, the introduction of this new service by KLM was a very welcome development.

In the autumn of 1968 a couple of newcomers were seen at Glasgow which would feature heavily in the airport's history, right up to the present day. At the end of September a DHC-6 Twin Otter CF-WTE acted as a demonstrator to BEA and flew a number of flights to the Highlands and Islands to demonstrate its capabilities. The first visit of a Boeing 737 came on 14 October when G-AVRM of Britannia Airways arrived on a demonstration flight from Newcastle and departed for its home base at Luton. Britannia was no stranger to Glasgow having landed there many times in its earlier guise as Euravia.

The Twin Otter was never bought by BEA, the state-owned airline opting for the Shorts Skyvan to replace its Heron aircraft from 1973. However, the Boeing 737 series, despite a slow start following its mid-1960s launch, went on to become the biggest selling airliner of all time with more than 6,000 having been ordered by 2008. It is worth noting that the 737s of today are vastly different beasts, excepting their general layout, to the Britannia and Lufthansa 737s of forty years ago.

Another new international service started on 2 November 1968 when Caravelle SE-DAG flew the first service for SAS to Copenhagen. This was to be three flights a week in winter and four in summer. SAS had already announced in March 1968 that they were transferring their operation from Prestwick to Abbotsinch in the autumn. SAS also alternated the use of Caravelles with their new DC9-40 with LN-RLC operating the service on 17 December 1968 and becoming the first DC9 to visit Abbotsinch. The first attempt at a Copenhagen to Glasgow service by BEA from Renfrew had ended due to a lack of demand. However, the SAS service carried good load factors. Perhaps the austere immediate post-war years were not the best time to start international services – certainly not from regional airports.

Donaldson International Airways had been formed in 1964 as a subsidiary of Waverly Shipping. Mercury Holidays was owned and financed by Waverly and Donaldson and, as previously mentioned, were flown by Lloyd International. For the summer 1968 a Donaldson Britannia (one of two ex-BUA Britannias) was used out of Glasgow for the season after being dry-leased to Lloyd International and operated in their livery. But after six years of operation by Lloyd International, Donaldson took over the summer season flights for 1969. The

The original terminal building after the first extensions had been carried out in the 1970s and early '80s. (Glasgow Airport Aviation Enthusiasts Club)

Tarom Ilyushin IL 18 YR-IMC taxiing with the outer engines closed down. In the 1990s she was preserved at Baneasa next to Romanian aviator Aurel Vlaico's monument. The Mayor of Baneasa ordered the aircraft to be dismantled and scrapped after children playing on it fell and seriously injured themselves. (Hugh Brown)

Donaldson International livery and interior design of their aircraft was by Glasgow-based interior designer Libby MacLean.

On 6 November 1968 British Eagle went into liquidation (the news being greeted with cheers from the Labour benches when it was announced in the House of Commons) thus removing a thorn in the side for the state-owned airlines BEA and BOAC.

By the end of 1968 the Loganair fleet had grown to six aircraft: two BN Islanders, a Skyvan, Piper Aztec B, Beech E18S and a Bolkow Junior. Loganair continued to expand with the arrival of Short Skyvan G-AWYG on 4 March 1969. The new Skyvan was put into service three days later with a flight to Stornoway. The airline's Beech E18S, registered G-ASUG, was put into service in May 1969 after an extensive modification and refit programme. It was the only example of its type in scheduled service in Europe. A second model arrived for Loganair on 12 December 1969: Beech C-45H N15662 (ex-RCAF 1566). The aircraft arrived by road and was intended only as a source of spares for earlier aircraft.

Three unusual visitors arrived from Turnhouse on 14 April 1969. They were Alitalia DC9 I-DIZA accompanied by Italian Air Force aircraft Convair CV440 MM61901 and Douglas DC6 MM61922. The aircraft were connected to an official visit by the President of Italy, Giuseppe Saragat.

During the 1969 summer season Balkan Bulgarian Airlines operated holiday charter flights to Varna on the Black Sea coast using IL18s LZ-BES, BED, BEV, BET and BEM.

The first visit of an Aer Lingus Boeing 737 was EI-ASA on 9 August 1969. Aer Lingus were gradually replacing their Viscounts on the Dublin route with a mixture of the new Boeing 737s and BAC1-11s.

During the winter season of 1969/70 Caledonian Airways started a new Sunday service to Palma which was flown on behalf of Global Holidays from 19 October 1969 until 26 April 1970. The first flight was undertaken by BAC1-11-500 G-AWWY.

After the start of their freighter service the previous year KLM decided to add a twice weekly DC9 passenger service to Amsterdam from November 1969. From the beginning KLM adopted the US 'hub and spoke' system where two points in Europe could be connected via their Amsterdam hub, a strategy which still works very well for KLM. The streamlined layout and easy transfer system available at Amsterdam Airport was extensively redeveloped shortly before the Glasgow service was introduced.

In 1969 Channel Airways had applied to the ATLB to operate a London (Stansted)–Glasgow service (among others) but were turned down. Following this, BUA applied for permission to increase its frequency on the Gatwick–Glasgow route, along with Edinburgh and Belfast, and this was granted.

One of the more unusual charter flights into Abbotsinch in 1969 was an IL18 YR-IMI of the Romanian airline TAROM which arrived on 2 December 1969 from Rotterdam with a consignment of tomatoes. This was to be the first of a number of irregular flights over the next few years from Rotterdam. Tarom would return on a regular basis as the 1970s boom in IT flights extended to Glasgow.

On 25 October 1970 the last round trip on BEA's Glasgow–Manchester–Palma Trident service took place before the route was dropped, although BEA was committed to providing all-jet services from provincial airports to the continent. In 1970 these included twice-daily BAC1-11-500 services from Glasgow to Dusseldorf via Manchester and Paris via Birmingham.

Unusually, on 5 February 1970 a Thai Airways Caravelle HS-TGF was seen. However, there was a fairly mundane explanation for its presence: it had just returned less than a week before from a seven-year lease to Thai Airways by SAS, and was now operating the normal SAS schedule to Copenhagen.

In late 1969 Balkan Bulgarian Airlines had planned to lease Tupolev TU-104 aircraft from the Russian state carrier Aeroflot to operate on holiday charter flights out of Glasgow for the 1970 summer season, but the lease did not come into fruition, and after sister airline Bulair had successfully operated IL18 summer flights to Varna in 1969 they returned for the following year. In 1971 there were no flights, but in 1972 Balkan supplanted Bulair using TU134s

BEA Vickers Viscount G-AOHI took off from Abbotsinch on 19 January 1973 on a test flight after work was carried out on the aircraft. The Viscount crashed on Ben More, near Crianlarich, with the tragic loss of four crew members. A memorial was erected to those who lost their lives and can be seen in the village of Crianlarich. (John Martindale)

initially before introducing the brand new TU154 on some of its first flights outside of the Soviet Union.

Wallace Arnold was a tour operator which used four Channel Airways Comets out of Glasgow for the summer 1970 season. They were G-APYC, G-APYD, G-APZM and G-ARDI. By 1970 Southend based Channel Airways was having financial troubles, incurring a heavy loss (amongst other losses) on its innovative Scottish Flyer Service (which comprised of eleven stops starting at Southend and going to Edinburgh and Aberdeen, not Glasgow). Its traditional cross-Channel routes faced stiff competition and the airline was looking to move into other areas of which the Wallace Arnold IT flights were one. Channel Airways Viscounts had been regular visitors into Abbotsinch and Renfrew, but the airline eventually folded in early 1972. As if to comment on the airline's state an aside made by an observer at Abbotsinch in 1970 expressed how 'tatty' the ex-Olympic Airways Channel Comets looked – a sad end for an airline which had once displayed a picture at its Southend base of a Concorde in the Channel Airways livery.

Britannia Airways operated a full schedule of IT flights from Abbotsinch in the 1970 summer season with flights to Alicante, Barcelona, Gerona, Ibiza, Palma and Venice. Their Boeing 737 fleet had grown to eight by 1970, and bases had been established at Gatwick, Manchester, Luton and Glasgow.

Two visitors on 19 May 1970 were Twin Otter CF-YFT and a Saunders ST-27 CF-XOK which both arrived to give demonstrations to BEA as part of the airline's continuing search for a replacement for their de Havilland Herons. The Saunders ST-27 was the basic frame of a DH Heron which had previously belonged to the Queen's Flight and had been reworked into CF-XOK, twin turboprop, twenty-four passenger airliner providing valid competition for the Twin Otter and Beech 99. However, neither type suited BEA and the decision was delayed.

One airline which made a striking visual impression wherever their BAC1-11s and Lockheed Tristars went was Court Line. The airline had originally been Autair International until Court Line Shipping took a controlling interest in 1969 and reshaped it into a holiday charter airline. They began operating IT flights from their base at Luton and other UK regional airports. Their BAC1-11s first appeared at Abbotsinch in July 1970 in their garish colours (all pink/turquoise/orange/lilac) so that each aircraft stood out from the other aircraft around them. It was reported that the first arrival of a Court Line BAC1-11 at its Luton base had prompted an air traffic controller to radio the aircraft to ask, 'Can I have a lick?'

D-ANUE BAC 1-11-528FL Bavaria Fluggesellschaft. Bavaria merged with Germanair in 1979, and then became Hapag Lloyd shortly after. D-ANUE ended its days flying as YR-JBB with Rumanian operator Jaro International, and was broken up in 2006. (John Martindale)

On 1 August 1970 a BOAC Boeing 747-100 G-AWNC made a low approach and overshot the runway. It was the first visit of a 747 but it did not land due to the restricted runway length. The largest aircraft to visit so far in the airport's short history arrived just over a month later when KLM Douglas DC8-63 PH-DEK arrived on 11 September 1970.

The first visit of a BEA Trident 3 was on 13 January 1971 when G-AWZA arrived from Heathrow. The Trident 3 had a greater passenger capacity than the two earlier Trident versions and would feature strongly at Abbotsinch until the introduction of the Boeing 757. Indeed, Glasgow and Edinburgh featured indirectly in the development of the Trident 3 since their restricted runway lengths necessitated higher power from the Trident's Spey engines. Rolls-Royce, together with the manufacturer Hawker Siddeley, offered a unique solution: a small turbojet located in the tail used to provide extra power for take-off. This helped shorten the take-off run, as the Trident was a notoriously poor performer in this regard.

BEA retired its Comets in 1971 with the last Comet G-APMA seen occasionally at Glasgow until its retirement on 31 October 1971. On the cargo side BEA introduced a pallet service from a number of domestic airports, including Glasgow, to improve the service to Europe, with the cargo transiting through the London airports. This saw the commencement of a weeknight cargo service using a converted Vickers Vanguard freighter, rebranded 'Merchantman'. The venerable Vanguard was never the quietest of airliners as the large Rolls-Royce Tynes developed a distinctive shrill noise at all speeds, and the noise travelled much further in the night air. One resident in Renfrew recalls that the Merchantman usually departed between 21.30 and 22.30 (local time), just after he had gone to bed as a schoolboy. Anyone dozing off to sleep was soon disturbed as the running up of Tynes could be heard even before it began taxiing to the threshold of runway 24!

March 1971 saw an invasion of Dutch aircraft from KLM, Transavia, Martinair and Moormanair when twenty-four aircraft arrived (including four DC8-63s). There were only three UK aircraft chartered for the Ajax FC/Celtic game in Glasgow.

Dan Air was already a regular visitor to the airport, but on 1 June 1971 they started their first scheduled flight into Glasgow from Leeds/Bradford with Hs748 G-ARAY, recently bought from Maersk, undertaking the first flight.

A second Boeing 747 G-AWNE made another overshoot on 2 June 1971. Five days later a Lockheed Tristar N301EA of the US Eastern Airlines also made an overshoot followed by a

Glasgow apron view: two Transavia Caravelles, one BMA BAC 1-11 and one KLM Douglas DC9, on 24 March 1971. (John Martindale)

flypast – the primary reason for the visit being a demonstration to Rolls-Royce employees at nearby Hillington, who were involved in making parts for the new RB211 high bypass engine. A Lockheed Tristar had also yet to land at Abbotsinch at this stage. At the other end of the scale, a Britten Norman Trislander paid its first visit on 13 June 1971 for a demonstration to Loganair. The demonstration was successful and Loganair went on to operate a number of the type on their island services.

BUA and Caledonian Airways merged in November 1970, using a temporary livery and title (BUA/Caledonian). This was changed to the new livery which showed the Caledonian Lion on the tail and the title 'British Caledonian' of the new airline on the fuselage. The first aircraft to display this new scheme was BAC1-11 G-ASJF which flew in on 29 October 1971. All the aircraft were given names, with G-ASJF bearing the name *Burgh of Ft William*. 1971 was obviously the year for new liveries: the two BEA Herons were painted in new colours, plus KLM and Britannia Airways flew aircraft into Abbotsinch during the year bearing new liveries.

Loftleidir also made a change on their service by replacing the CL44s with Douglas DC8-55CFs, and later DC-8-63 aircraft. The last service into Abbotsinch by a Loftleidir CL44 was TF-LLF on 5 November 1971 with DC8-54 TF-LLK taking over the weekly service to Keflavik and New York from Abbotsinch on 13 November.

The main event at the airport in 1972 was the completion of work carried out to extend the main runway 06/24 from 6,720ft (2,048m) to 8,419ft (2,566m), opened to traffic on 29 June 1972. This enabled larger and heavier aircraft to operate. The runway was also resurfaced during the year and Edinburgh became the beneficiary of an increase in European charter traffic whilst the runway work was being carried out at Abbotsinch. The runway was later shown in landing charts as 8,720ft (2,658m), which included the 300ft (91m) turning area at the eastern end of the main runway (then runway 24). The ILS was also upgraded to Category III standard, becoming the first airport in the UK after Heathrow to have this facility.

Another foreign carrier to start services from Abbotsinch was Lufthansa. As with other European services from Glasgow the new service to Frankfurt ran via Manchester. Boeing 737-100 D-ABEO flew the first flight on 4 April 1972. By December 1972 the whole of Lufthansa's fleet of Boeing 737s had flown this route at some point. The early Lufthansa-200 aircraft were

QC frames used for night freight services in Europe, and they only occasionally appeared at Glasgow as substitutes for Lufthansa-100 aircraft.

Balkan Bulgarian Airlines introduced the Tupolev TU154 in place of its IL18s for its summer IT flights in 1972. The first visit by a TU154 to Abbotsinch was LZ-BTA on 2 July 1972. Balkan had also started using TU134s on their IT flights as well.

Another airline replacing aircraft at the time was Iberia which was phasing out its Caravelles and replacing them with the Douglas DC9. The first Iberia DC9 to fly into Glasgow was EC-BIP (A DC9-32) on 9 September 1972.

A significant first time visitor on 17 September 1972 was a Lockheed Tristar of Eastern Airlines. This was the first time one of the new 'widebody' aircraft had visited. The Tristar was on a demonstration tour and had BEA markings on its forward fuselage and tail. The arrival of the next 'widebody' aircraft took place shortly after the visit of the Tristar when Laker Airways DC10 G-AZZC arrived on 24 November 1972 with another Laker Airways DC10 (G-AZZD) making an overshoot on 5 December 1972. Tristars and DC10s were never regular visitors to Abbotsinch until the mid-1980s when British Caledonian Charter used DC10s on high-density European charters. When Glasgow achieved transatlantic gateway status in 1990 British Airways, American Airlines and later Continental used them on scheduled services.

One charter airline which made its first visit to Glasgow with Boeing 720 G-AZKM on 7 November 1972 was Monarch Airlines. A second Monarch Boeing 720 G-AZFB visited on 25 November 1972. Monarch Airlines is still operating with the same name and more or less the same basic colour scheme (albeit with newer aircraft) thirty-seven years later – which is quite an achievement in the fast moving and somewhat volatile world of charter airlines.

By 1972 the two BEA Herons (G-ANXA and G-ANXB) had been serving the Highlands and Islands for seventeen years and it was felt that it was time to replace them. The requirement for a replacement had certain specifications which needed to be met: the aircraft would need to have fixed undercarriages rather than retractable ones, due to the salt and sand on the beach at Barra which would corrode the relatively complex and delicate mechanism of retractable undercarriages. BEA decided to place an order for three Britten Norman Trislanders. However, the manufacturer of the Trislander, Britten-Norman, was having serious financial difficulties in 1972 and the order was never confirmed by BEA. BEA decided to place an order in 1972 for two Short Skyliners instead, and they were delivered in 1973.

British Caledonian BAC 1-11 G-AYOP with the BEA Engineering Hangar in the background. Sold to Savannah Airlines as 5N-BDV and later stored at Maiduguri in Nigeria. (John Martindale)

BEA withdrew the first class facility on their Tridents and Vanguards to Heathrow on 31 March 1973. For a £2 supplement seats were available on both types of aircraft which had extra leg-room. This went some way toward alleviating the withdrawal of their first class facilities.

The last scheduled service to be operated by a BEA Heron was on 30 March 1973 when G-ANXB flew the Barra–Tiree–Glasgow sector for the last time. Skyliners took over on 1 April 1973 and the two Herons were withdrawn, overhauled and stored at Abbotsinch pending their sale. Short Skyliner G-AZYW arrived and took up residence on 8 March 1973, followed by G-BAIT on 20 April 1973. G-AZYW operated the type's first commercial service on 2 April when it flew the Glasgow–Tiree route. With the arrival of G-BAIT the two Skyliners took over the routes previously operated by Herons. The two Herons were both sold to Peters Aviation at Norwich later that year. Despite having given good service the economics of operating the Herons had not been good for BEA. It was calculated that the aircraft required a 125 per cent load factor to break even on its operating costs. So, in other words, it needed three more passengers than it could carry (the maximum passenger load was fourteen) in order to break even. The Skyliners only lasted four years before they were withdrawn and eventually sold in Norway. The other requirement for the Herons had been the provision of the air ambulance service from Glasgow. On 1 April 1973, following a decision by the Secretary of State for Scotland, Loganair became entirely responsible for the operation of the Scottish air ambulance service.

Loganair's Skyvan displayed its new colours on 5 March 1973. Later that month, on 23 March, the Loganair Beech 18 G-ASUG also displayed new colours along with a new executive interior. On 9 June 1973 they took delivery of their first BN Trislander.

The first visit by a Court Line Lockheed Tristar came on 27 March 1973 when G-BAAA arrived on a demonstration flight, showing off its garish yellow colour.

BAA carried on discussions with Glasgow Corporation 1973/74 with a view to the eventual takeover of the airport. The third Boeing 747-100 of BOAC to visit Abbotsinch was G-AWNM on 10 May 1973. Again, the 747 did not land as such but made two ILS approaches and one touch and go.

Loganair sold their Skyvan G-AWYG to the USA and also increased the Glasgow–Skye service from three to six a week from December 1973.

After eighteen months of operation Lufthansa announced in September 1973 that their Glasgow–Manchester–Frankfurt service would be withdrawn the following month.

The RAF was a regular visitor to Abbotsinch with various aircraft including Britannias and Hs748s during this period. The first RAF VC10 to visit was XV102 on 8 July 1972, shortly after the runway extension was completed.

British Island Airways started a new service to Dublin with Handley Page Herald G-BAZJ on 2 November 1973.

There were a number of unusual visitors (in aircraft and passengers) in 1973 worthy of mention. On 15 June IL18 OK-PAE Czechoslovakian Airlines arrived for a fuel stop. The Czech airline was a rare visitor into Glasgow. On 27 June 1973 Fokker F28 Fellowship D-AHLA of Aviaction arrived bringing in the Brazilian football team for a friendly match. Another Eastern European visitor on 10 September was Tupolev TU134 DM-SCH of the East German airline Interflug. Although they had visited before with IL18s this was the first visit of a TU134 by this airline. The singer Diana Ross arrived on 28 September in Martinair DC9-32 PH-MAO, and lastly, LAN Chile Boeing 707 CC-CEA passed through on 14 December.

The British Airports Authority (BAA) carried on discussions with Glasgow Corporation in 1973/74 with a view to the eventual takeover of the airport. The BAA had taken over control of Edinburgh back in 1971 and was working to bring Turnhouse up to a decent standard, and wished to do the same for Abbotsinch.

By 1974, apart from Aer Lingus, the international operators of scheduled services were represented by the stalwarts at Glasgow: KLM and Icelandair, along with SAS. Additionally, Loftleidir the Icelandic airline operated a scheduled DC8 service to Reykjavik and New York. KLM flew a passenger and cargo service to Amsterdam using a DC9 whilst Icelandair operated a Boeing 727 from Reyjavik to Copenhagen routed through Glasgow.

F–BVUY Vickers V952 Vanguard of Europe Air Service taxis in past an Air Charter International Caravelle on 12 May 1976. (Charlie Stewart)

Much in evidence were British Airways as Glasgow was the only airport where their full range of fixed wing aircraft could be seen, ranging from the Trident 3 to the 'Merchantman' and Skyliner. Scottish Airways, a division of the British Airways regional network, also had their headquarters at the airport.

Lufthansa had withdrawn from Glasgow at the end of the previous year but this was some-what offset by the introduction of two new services. The first was a new all-cargo service by Swissair. Swissair had been flying into Glasgow on an irregular basis over the years with Caravelles and latterly with DC9s. The new cargo service to Zurich via Manchester departed from Glasgow at 03.25 on Wednesday, Thursday, Friday and Saturday, with DC9 HB-IFW undertaking the first flight on 2 May 1974. The second new service started on 1 April 1975 when SAS began a Glasgow–Stavanger–Oslo service.

The Inclusive Tour market was well covered and mention of the airlines and aircraft gives a flavour of the time: Air Spain (DC8), Aviaco (Caravelle), Spantax (Convair 990 Coronado), Balkan Bulgarian (TU154), Braathens-Safe (Boeing 737, F27), Britannia Airways (Boeing 737), British Airtours (Boeing 707), British Caledonian (BAC1-11), Court Line (BAC1-11), Dan Air (Boeing 727), Donaldson International (Boeing 707), Iberia (DC8), Inex Adria (DC9), Sterling Airways (Caravelle) and Tarom (IL62).

There were, however, to be two noticeable absentees from the IT airlines after 1974/75. On 31 March 1974 BAC1-11 G-AXMG made its last flight into Abbotsinch for Court Line as the airline went into liquidation later in the year on 15 August 1974 along with its associated in-house tour operator, Clarksons. The second was Air Spain which made its last flight to the airport on 4 October 1974 with DC8 EC-CAD, operating flight No. JA166, before they ceased operations in 1975 after merger talks with Aviaco broke down.

In September 1974, an announcement was made that an agreement had been reached between the BAA and Glasgow Corporation. BAA would take over Abbotsinch on 1 April 1975 and would cover the current debt of £6.25 million and pay Glasgow Corporation £1 million. This agreement was reached during the Oil Crisis of 1973/74, which had led to a downturn in traffic figures. Despite this economic downturn the continual growth in air travel was out-stripping the capacity of the facilities to cope with it. The decrease in traffic because of the Oil

Court Line Lockheed L1011-385-1 Tristar 1 G-BAAA on 27 March 1973. This was the first Tristar to be based in Europe, and went on to fly with Cathay Pacific for twenty years as VR-HHV from 1977 on. Court Line is fondly remembered by many. (John Martindale)

Saturn Airways Hercules N15ST on 31 December 1976. The Hercules had brought in a propeller shaft for the *QE2*. (Glasgow Airport Aviation Enthusiasts Club)

Crisis had caused the shelving of plans to build a star shaped terminal for 'widebody' aircraft between stands 4 and 10. The slowdown was merely a temporary lull.

Some notable visitors during 1974 were: Athletico Madrid who arrived in Aviaco DC8 EC-ARC on 7 April; the singer David Cassidy arriving on Transavia Caravelle PH–TRO on 24 May; Boeing 707 YR-ABA which was the first visit of a TAROM Boeing 707 on 1 June; Boeing 707 9M-ATR which passed through on 14 July and was the first visit by MAS–Malaysian Airline System; and the first visit of a British Airways Tristar G-BBAE on 4 November 1974. BA Tristars started to fly into Glasgow on a quite frequent basis after this first visit. G-BBAE itself made another three visits before the end of the year. The first 'proper' visit by a Boeing 747 was on 15 May 1974 when a BA747, G-AWNM, in BOAC colours, successfully landed.

Central Scotland Airport and the Turnhouse Inquiry

After the longest planning inquiry in Scottish history approval was finally given in 1974 for the redevelopment of Turnhouse, which necessitated a new runway and terminal building. During the inquiry the principal objectors to the expansion of Turnhouse (the Cramond Association) had raised the idea of a Central Scotland Airport. Their proposal was to close all three lowland airports (Glasgow, Edinburgh and Prestwick) and replace them with one airport with an 11,000ft runway in the central Lowlands. Airth was suggested as a possible location. The idea was rejected by the inquiry, but G.S. Gimson QC, the reporter, felt the proposal had merit and deserved further examination.

BAA Assume Ownership

Ownership of Glasgow Airport officially passed from Glasgow Corporation to the Scottish Airports Division of the BAA on 1 April 1975. Despite industrial action (an electricians' strike) which caused the closure of the airport for almost five weeks prior to the takeover, the airport returned to full operation on 3 April 1975. The Scottish Airports Division itself came into being on 1 April 1975, with its headquarters at Glasgow Airport, and was responsible for the development, operation and management of Glasgow, Prestwick, Edinburgh and Aberdeen airports. At the time of the takeover by the BAA, Glasgow found itself in the same position as Edinburgh in relation to Prestwick. The BAA stated at the time that an historical accident had bequeathed three fine Lowland airports with a capacity far greater than could be expected within the decade. They were jointly capable of handling three times their current combined traffic of 3.4 million passengers per annum.

Following a visit to the three airports by Clinton Davis, the Parliamentary Secretary of State for Companies, Aviation and Shipping, the BAA issued a policy statement on the role of the three Lowland airports which confirmed the traditional arrangement. Prestwick was to continue handling long-haul intercontinental flights while Edinburgh and Glasgow airports catered for short- and medium-haul domestic and European flights.

At the end of 1975 the first stage of the terminal building improvement programme was begun with work starting on the new domestic baggage reclaim hall which was double the size of the existing area.

The introduction of the Shuttle concept by British Airways on the Heathrow–Glasgow route was a major boost to passenger numbers. The new service was launched on 12 January 1975 with Trident 1 G-ARPC making the first flight. Once the service was fully operational the intention was to have the Trident 3, with its greater passenger capacity, operate the schedules, with back up provided by the smaller Trident 1. By Friday of the first week 10,000 passengers had been carried. As mentioned earlier, the idea for a London Shuttle had been mooted by BEA in 1962. Basically, provided a passenger turned up on time, they were guaranteed a seat

1 British Eagle DH Dove 5, G-AROI, on 12 June 1967. It operated the twice-daily Glasgow–Dundee service from 5 July 1966 until the route was dropped on 31 October 1967 after the airline incurred losses of £10,000 on the route. (John Martindale)

2 Interflug DM-SEF Ilyushin IL-62 arriving on 29 August 1976 – the first visit of an IL-62. Now on display at Aero Park Museum in Leipzig-Halle. (Hugh Brown)

3 BEA DH Heron 1B, G-ANXA, stands in the early evening sun of 24 April 1968, awaiting another ambulance call. (John Martindale)

4 Loganair's first 'airliner' Piper PA-23-250 Aztec G-ARMH at Renfrew in May 1964. (Gordon Reid)

5 Dutch Air Force KDC-10 T-235 brought in troops for an exercise on 13 February 2006 and returned a week later to pick them up. It is stationed at Eindhoven Airport with T-264 as part of RNAF 334 Transport Squadron. The Dutch KDC-10s are used for transportation and refuelling. (Fred Seggie)

6 N736T Aeroamerica Boeing 720-027 visited in August and September 1978, operating flights on behalf of Britannia Airways, whose aircraft were affected by the French ATC strike that year. (Glasgow Airport Aviation Enthusiasts Club)

7 Czech Airlines Boeing 737-55S OK-DGL on 24 March 2005 painted in a special livery for the eightieth anniversary of the airline. (Fred Seggie)

8 A6-EBA Boeing 777-31H-ER of Emirates Airways on 28 February 2006 makes an impressive take-off against the stunning backdrop of the Kilpatrick Hills. (Fred Seggie)

9 Mexican Casa 212s were present on 22–24 March 1986. The scene looks like the apron of a Mexican Naval Air Base. MP111 went to 1 Escuadron Aeronaval at Chetumal in Quintana Roo Province and the remainder to 3 Escuadron Aeronaval at Veracruz and 4 Escuadron Aeronaval at La Paz, Baja–California Province, Mexico. (Gerry McLaughlin)

10 12 May 1976. Icelandair Boeing 727 TF-FIE taxies in alongside an Air France Boeing 747 and a Catair Caravelle, both of which brought in supporters for the Bayern Munich V St Etienne football match. International Air Bahama DC-8-63CF N8630 is nearly obscured from view. Up to that point, this was the busiest day in the airport's history. (Glasgow Airport Aviation Enthusiasts Club)

11 Court Line BAC 1-11-518FG, G-AXMF, on 24 March 1971, with KLM DC 8-63 PH-DEG and a Transavia SE210 Caravelle PH-TRS, all of which arrived with football fans for the Ajax FC V Celtic match. Note the Court Line air hostess in the bottom right of the picture wearing the Mary Quant-designed uniform. (John Martindale)

12 Among the aircraft on display at RNAS Abbotsinch 'Air Day' on 8 July 1961 were Hawker Hunter T.8 XF289 '707/LM' of 764 Squadron, RNAS Lossiemouth, and Grumman SA.16B Albatross 15287 of 67th ARS USAF, based at Prestwick. (Douglas A. Rough)

13 At RAF Abbotsinch in July 1961 was this impressive line-up of eighteen Hawker Sea Hawks awaiting scrapping. They included WM991, an Armstrong Whitworth-built FB.3. Prior to its operational service it was delivered 'as new' to AHU Abbotsinch from the manafacturer's airfield at Bitteswell on 17 August 1954. (Douglas A. Rough)

14 Boeing 707-351C YU-AGJ, a regular summer visitor from 1980 to 1986. After the break up of Yugoslavia in 1992, JAT only operated a few domestic services. The Serbian airline was renamed JAT Airways on 8 August 2003, with the other states operating their own airlines. (Hugh Brown)

15 Vickers Viscount 812, G–AVHE, of Channel Airways on 18 June 1970. Channel Airways had acquired eleven Viscounts from the US airline Continental in the late 1960s. The only item changed in the livery appears to be the name. (John Martindale)

16 Olympic Airways DH Comet 4B, SX-DAL on 25 July 1968. This Comet went on to serve Channel Airways and Dan-Air. It is now preserved in the Science Museum at Wroughton. (John Martindale)

17 Grob 115E Tutor TMk.1 G-BYVD of the University of Glasgow and Strathclyde Air Squadron (UGSAS) on 5 January 2009. Formed as Glasgow University Air Squadron on 13 January 1942, the squadron recruited from Glasgow University and was involved in pre-training pilots for the RAF. Equipped with Tiger Moths and Miles Magisters after the war, the squadron temporarily moved to Scone before returning to Abbotsinch. The name was altered to include Strathclyde University in 1965, and today the squadron has approximately fifty student officer cadets who are members of the RAFVR. (Douglas Rough Collection)

18 Into the wind: G-BZFP DHC 6-300 Twin Otter landing from Barra on 26 March 2009 in a 37-knot crosswind. Flybe took over BA's regional operation in October 2008, hence the franchise tie-in with Loganair. (Fred Seggie)

19 From time to time the airport received visitors in connection with the Rolls-Royce factory at East Kilbride. One unusual visitor in this respect arrived on 1 December 1981: Fokker F28-1000C Fellowship TU-VAB, belonging to the government of the Ivory Coast, bringing in three engines for overhaul. (Gerry McLaughlin)

20 DH Dove 6s G-ARMT and G-AMZY with a Cambrian Airways Viscount on the apron at Renfrew. (Gordon Reid)

21 16 July 2008: celebrating ten years of operations at Glasgow, Continental Airlines Boeing 757-224 N14115 is given a 'Fire Hose Salute'. (Fred Seggie)

22 Boeing 717-23S HS-PGP of Bangkok Airways was the star movement of 2007, passing through on its return to Miami from Thailand at the end of its lease, 11 December 2007. (Fred Seggie)

23 BCAL CommuterViscount 806, G-AOYR, leased by BCAL from March 1985 to May 1986 from British Air Ferries.This was the second livery used by BCAL during its lease. G-AOYR was broken up at Southend in 1996. (Gerry MacLaughlin)

24 PIA Airbus A-310-308, AP-BEU, 2 April 2004.The return of PIA to Glasgow. (Kevin Marchbank)

25 BEA DH Trident 2 G-AVFF, 7 June 1969. Parked on Stand 1, this was the Birmingham evening flight and had just arrived from Birmingham (originating in mainland Europe and returning to Birmingham). Trident 2s were not regular Glasgow visitors, tending to be used on European Mainland routes. (John Martindale)

26 Firecat F-WEOL in October 1995. It first flew with the US Navy as Grumman S2F-1 Tracker 136552. It was passing through on its way to Conair in Canada to have its reciprocating engines replaced by turbines. On its return as an air tanker for the Securite Civile it was re-registered F-ZBMA and designated Tanker No.24. (Fred Seggie)

27 Derby Airways Canadair C4 Argonaut G-ALHS at Renfrew in May 1964. An ex-BOAC aircraft, it was finally broken up in 1970. (Gordon Reid)

28 Hispania Lineas Aereas Sud Est SE.2106R Caravelle EC-DCN on 9 May 1986. On some days all three Hispania Caravelles would visit during the peak holiday season. Founded in 1982, the airline ceased operations in July 1989 due to financial difficulties. (Gerry Mclaughlin)

29 BEA DH Comet 4B G-ARJK taxies past an Aer Lingus Viscount on 16 April 1969 with the tail of a Lufthansa Boeing 737 visible on the other side of the then International Pier. (John Martindale)

30 Iberia Boeing 747-256B EC-BRQ operating a Tuesday night flight to Tenerife on 26 March 1986. This was the oldest Boeing 747 in Iberia's fleet and was finally scrapped at Madrid-Barajas in May 2003. (Dr Alastair T. Gardner)

31 Lockheed L1011-385 Tristar C-GTSP of Air Transat on 19 April 2003, originally delivered to TAP on 19 June 1983 as CS-TED before being bought by Air Transat in April 1997. (Fred Seggie)

32 Spantax Convair CV 990-A Coronado EC-BZO, a classic airliner. Only thirty-seven were built, despite it being the fastest subsonic commercial airliner of its time. It is identifiable by the pods on the wings, known after their designer Dietrich Kuchemann as 'Kuchemann Carrots', which were anti-shock bodies to reduce transonic drag. (Glasgow Airport Aviation Enthusiasts Club)

Interflug TU 134 DM-SCL on 8 July 1979. Interflug aircraft came to bring in and take home fishing fleet crews. DM-SCL was later bought by aircraft ground support equipment manufacturer Hydro-Gertebau GmbH and preserved on land outside their offices in Biberach/Baden. (Glasgow Airport Aviation Enthusiasts Club)

even if a back-up aircraft had to be provided for a single passenger. Despite a few teething problems, British Airways carried 64,500 passengers on the route in September 1975, which was a 23 per cent increase on the same route in the same month of the previous year when a more conventional, pre-booked service was operating. Indications showed that overall the shuttle concept continued to generate between 15 per cent and 20 per cent more traffic than otherwise would have been carried.

Loganair's Beech 18 G-ASUG made its last commercial flight on 11 January 1975. On that same day a British Airways Super VC 10 G-ASGF made its first visit.

In February 1974, British Airways/BEA had placed an order for two Hs748-2As to be used on its Scottish services. They were both to be based at Glasgow with the first, G-BCOE, arriving on 10 July 1975, and the second, G-BCOF, arriving on 3 September 1975.

Football visitors during 1975 included three British Airways Tristars G-BBAE, G-BBAG and G-BBAJ for an England/Scotland match on 25 May, and TAROM IL18s YR-IMD and YR-IMI on 15 and 18 December for a Rumania/Scotland match at Hampden. It must have made quite a change for these IL18s to be carrying football supporters between Bucharest and Glasgow as opposed to carrying tomatoes between Rotterdam and Glasgow.

During the 1976/77 period, the average overall growth in passengers for the four BAA Scottish airports was almost 11 per cent, with no apparent trend towards the use of larger aircraft. This was greater than that at the three London airports. Passenger traffic at Glasgow, however, was down by 0.4 per cent. This was due to a number of factors; a reflection in the slump in the UK's Inclusive Tour business, a greater reliability of Edinburgh with the opening of the new runway meaning fewer diversions to Glasgow, the extension of the British Airways shuttle service from Heathrow to Edinburgh which took some traffic from the Heathrow to Glasgow shuttle destined for Edinburgh. Two other factors which contributed to the decline were an unusually high number of days with dense fog causing diversions, along with an industrial dispute with firemen which closed the airport for seven days in February 1977.

One feature of this period was continuing concern over aircraft noise at all the BAA airports. Grants were made available to households which qualified for relief and, in addition, a summer

Air Malta Boeing 720 9H-AAN. This aircraft had been wet leased from Pakistan International Airlines (PIA) before being put on the Maltese register. Air Malta had been formed with the assistance of PIA, who originally owned 20 per cent of the share capital. (Glasgow Airport Aviation Enthusiasts Club)

quota for jets at Glasgow was put into effect. From 1 April 1977 to 31 October 1977 the quota allowed 2,000 night jet movements between 23.30 and 06.30 hours. Additionally, standard instrument departure routes were agreed which took into account environmental conditions, available navigational aids, safety and the future concept of airspace utilisation.

By 1977/78 various parties were starting to press for a change to the status of the three Lowland airports in relation to the traffic they handled, moves that would ultimately be to the detriment of Prestwick.

The Glasgow Airport Committee on the other hand was concerned with the indiscriminate dumping of material at Rowand's Coup near to the airport perimeter. This material attracted large numbers of birds which were a hazard to aircraft landing and taking off. Action was taken through the district council to stop the owners of the site handling any material other than building materials and rubble, and eventually action was taken under the Town and County Planning Act which required the owners to remove all material and to soil and grass the Coup within a limited period. This action permanently removed the hazard to the aircraft.

On the airside of the airport a significant arrival on 24 February 1976 was Air Canada DC8-63 CF-TIL which arrived from Heathrow as flight No. AC853. The DC8 had been diverted from Prestwick as a result of a change to Air Canada's policy which now designated Abbotsinch as the official diversion airport instead of Prestwick. The DC8 took off for Winnipeg 3,599 miles away with 130 passengers on board, demonstrating that Abbotsinch was perfectly capable of handling transatlantic flights.

Loganair took delivery of their first new long-nosed version of the BN Trislander on 2 March 1976 when G-BCYC arrived to take up residence. On 9 May 1976 a DC3 N8009 belonging to Air Nashua landed at Abbotsinch in error! It should have landed at Prestwick and went there the following day.

During May there were also a large number of football related aircraft with Bavaria Fluggesellschaft BAC1-11 D-AMUC bringing in the Bayern Munich FC team plus a large contingent of aircraft from France, including the first visit by an Airbus A300 D-AMAY of

Britannia Airways Boeing 737-204 G-AVRO. One of the first batch of four Boeing 737s for Britannia. (Glasgow Airport Aviation Enthusiasts Club)

Laker Airways DC 10-10 'Skytrain' G-BBSZ, named *Canterbury Belle* after Freddie Laker's home town of Canterbury, Kent, making its first visit after being diverted from Prestwick on 22 September 1978. (Glasgow Airport Aviation Enthusiasts Club)

Germanair on 12 May. There were also three Boeing 747s, F-BPVF, F-BPVL of Air France and PH-BUI of KLM, which flew in supporters.

On 28 August 1976 Inex Adria DC9 YU-AJR made its last visit. It was destroyed over Zagreb thirteen days later when it collided with British Airways Trident 3 G-AWZT with the loss of 176 lives.

The first visit of an IL62 took place on 29 August 1976 when DM-SEF of East German airline Interflug arrived. It came back three days later on 1 September, and another IL62 arrived that same month when YR-IRA of TAROM visited on 19 September. Another first-time visit of an Eastern European visitor was YAK40 CCCP87490 of Russian state airline Aeroflot on 22 September 1976. Three notable 'heavy' visitors on 15 October 1976 were Alitalia DC8 I-DIWV, DC10 I-DYND and Boeing 747 I-DEMO. I-DYND was the first visit of a DC10 series 30. These Alitalia aircraft were involved in transporting passengers to Rome for the canonisation of John Ogilvie.

On the last day of 1976 Lockheed Hercules N15ST of freight carrier Saturn Airways arrived from Frankfurt bringing a propeller shaft for the *QE2*.

The spectators terrace was closed at the beginning of March 1977 to allow for alterations to the roof and buildings to continue unhindered for a period of four weeks. The terrace was reopened to spectators and then promptly closed again in June 1977 for a period scheduled for eighteen months while extension work was carried out on the international end of the terminal. However, the terrace would not subsequently re-open. Once this work was complete the terminal was then extended adjacent to the new baggage hall. Construction work was also scheduled to be carried out by British Airways to reconfigure their hangar to accommodate their Lockheed Tristars, but this did not happen and only much later was the hangar roof modified to accept Boeing 757s.

Loganair ordered a completely new type of aircraft, a DC6 Twin Otter, which arrived on 19 March 1977. In July 1977 the Spanish charter airline Aviaco was having capacity shortages. One of their DC8s was held over Glasgow for thirty minutes before permission was granted for it to land, leaving an outer engine running during turnaround to make for a speedier departure.

British Caledonian had applied for a licence in 1977 to operate a Glasgow–Newcastle–Paris (Charles De Gaulle) service, but this was turned down by the ATLB. An unusual service which started on 13 May 1977 was Burnthills Aviation Bell 206 weekday helicopter service to Fort William which later included stops at Rothesay, Lochgilphead and Oban. The service lasted until 1984.

Some significant visitors in 1977 were D-ABVI Boeing 727 of Condor which arrived on 20 March with the Stuttgart City Orchestra, HA-YSA TU 134 of the Hungarian Government on 9 May, and N408PA, a Pan Am Boeing 707 operated Aer Lingus flight EI224/5 to and from Dublin, on 3 August. This was a most unusual sight as the Boeing 707 had been leased by Aer Lingus due to their pilots striking over pay on 3 August. This was the first time a Pan American Airways aircraft had been seen at Glasgow. Aer Lingus also used one of their two Boeing 747s EI-ASI for a service on 22 October which was the first visit of its type for the airline.

Work continued throughout 1978 on the redevelopment of the terminal building which added, during peak periods, to a somewhat claustrophobic feel. A French air traffic controllers strike in August 1978 led Britannia Airways to use different operators to cover for aircraft affected by the strike, including Aeroamerica Boeing 720 N736T and Finnish operator Karair DC8 OH-KDM. Another airline which had to call upon another operator was Aer Lingus which leased two Montana Austria Boeing 707s (OE-IRA and OE-INA) to operate some of its flights in 1977/78, including the Dublin–Glasgow route.

A new holiday charter operator appeared at Glasgow in 1978 when Air Malta started Glasgow–Malta flights using a leased PIA (Pakistan International Airways) aircraft Boeing 720 AP-AMG. The first flight of the season was by flown by AP-AMG on 10 April 1978. Later that summer they used another leased (from Eagle Air of Iceland) Boeing 720 TF-VLC.

Loganair took delivery of a DHC6 Twin Otter on 30 March 1978 registered VP-FAW. This Twin Otter had previously belonged to the British Antarctic Survey.

Air Anglia Fokker F27 Friendship 200 G-BLGW. This aircraft was manufactured in 1963 and flew for a number of owners before being withdrawn from use in 1994. (Glasgow Airport Aviation Enthusiasts Club)

Aer Lingus BAC 1-11 EI-ANH, sold to Hold Trade Air of Nigeria in 1991 as 5N-HTB. (Malcolm Fife)

In May 1978 a first visit to the airport was made by a Dash 7 C-GNBX which arrived from Edinburgh on its way to Reykjavik. This was the prototype Dash 7 and it gave a demonstration for British Airways.

Despite the wide variety of different transport aircraft which used the airport, the dominance of two types (Tridents and BAC1-11s) was shown in the breakdown of statistics for 1978/79. The two aircraft types accounted for almost 40 per cent of total transport movements (19.4 per cent were Trident movements and 18.5 per cent were BAC1-11 movements).

The distribution of traffic through the three Lowland airports was once again called into question by Lothian Regional Council and British Airways. Lothian Council wanted direct transatlantic services to be allowed into Edinburgh and BA wished to see Glasgow airport developed as a hub airport and base for long-haul flights. Following a detailed review, a meeting was held on 19 December 1979 between Government Ministers at the Scottish Office and the Department of Trade along with representatives from BAA and British Airways. After the meeting the Department of Trade issued a statement which once again confirmed the status quo.

Although quieter aircraft were yet to come into general use at the start of the 1980s, the issue of aircraft noise was of great concern. Noise checks on all aircraft were already in place at the airport, and to supplement these regular checks a special three-month programme of aircraft noise movements was set in place during the midsummer of 1979. This was in order to validate noise forecasts which had been made three years earlier. Altogether 1,200 noise events were measured at nine elevated points covering a seven-mile flight path. The conclusion reached was that while the volume had increased, the forecast was reasonably accurate.

The major event at the end of the decade was the completion of the redevelopment of the terminal building. This was the finale of three years of redevelopment work to modernise the facilities. Since work had begun on the £2.5 million project in 1977, the check-in area had been trebled and a new aerogrill, shop and bar brought into use. A new buffet had been opened and the extended international departures lounge completed. Along with improvements to the duty free facilities, the airport was well placed to face the start of the 1980s.

Air Ecosse started two new services during 1979 which gave them a large boost. The first was a service carrying mail to Luton and Liverpool on a Royal Mail contract. The second was a direct Glasgow–Wick service. On 1 April 1980 they started three round trips a day on the Glasgow–Aberdeen service using Bandeirantes in competition with BA.

BIA (British Island Airways) started a return service to Exeter using Air Westward Titan G-WTVC and Navajo G-CITYs, but soon ordered Bandeirantes to replace them.

British Airways started a new Glasgow–Aberdeen–Shetland service in spring 1979.

Loganair became the first British operator to use Short 330s in July 1979.

1980–1990 – A Period of Recession and Growth

At the beginning of the 1980s the total number of passengers passing through Glasgow was on the decrease, in common with many other UK airports, due to the effects of the recession. The 1980/81 figure of 2,328,397 passengers was down 3.3 per cent on the previous year. However, the overall figure hid a more complex picture. There was a marked difference between scheduled services (down by 9 per cent) and charter services (up by nearly 14 per cent). On scheduled routes, domestic traffic decreased by 8.5 per cent and European scheduled traffic also decreased by 7.4 per cent. In contrast, however, European charter passengers rose by 24 per cent with particularly large increases being recorded by Greece (up 120 per cent), Portugal (up 175 per cent) and Malta (up 65 per cent). There was also a substantial drop in air cargo tonnage which was down by 23 per cent to 12,500 metric tons.

The continuing saga of Government policy towards the three lowland airports was in the news on 11 August 1980. Speaking at the start of a tour of BAA Scottish airports, the Parliamentary Under-Secretary of State, Norman Tebbit, made a statement which confirmed the complementary roles of the three airports, stating 'It is time that uncertainty about Prestwick is ended'.

Alitalia DC 10-30 I-DYND arrived on 15 October 1976 to take passengers to Rome for the canonisation of John Ogilvie, the Scottish Roman Catholic martyr who was hanged at Glasgow Cross on 10 March 1615. (Hugh Brown)

TAP Boeing 707 CS-TBE on 12 October 1979. This aircraft went on to TAAG Angolan Airlines as D2-TOP and was withdrawn from use in December 1998 at Luanda. (Hugh Brown)

He finished his statement with the words: 'Indeed, we look forward to Prestwick's continuing role as Scotland's main gateway international airport.' This statement was made with the failure of the Translink feeder service in the 1980 summer season due to inadequate demand in the background. The feeder service which linked Aberdeen and Edinburgh with Prestwick left Loganair with a significant loss, along with the loss to the BAA of the high passenger subsidy which they underwrote.

Runway 06/24 was re-designated 05/23 on 24 March 1981 with the new runway markings painted on the night of 23/24 March 1981. Additionally, the runway was closed for night operations throughout the spring months of 1981 in order to enable the airfield's entire lighting system to be re-cabled.

Air UK was formed on 16 January 1980 from Air Anglia and British Island Airways. The Navajos which had been used on the Glasgow–Teeside–Hull service and also on the Glasgow–Exeter route were replaced with Bandeirantes. The new airline dropped the Exeter route at the end of 1980. Air UK also operated a brief F27 mail contract from Glasgow to Stansted in the early part of 1980. Loganair's Glasgow–Skye and Glasgow–Tiree services were cut back during 1980. Loganair also took the decision to replace their BN Trislanders with DH Twin Otters. Icelandair abandoned its Luxembourg–Glasgow–Keflavik–New York JFK–Chicago route. This route had carried 300,000 passengers a year in its heyday but was now

Short SD.330 Var.100 G-BLTD Metropolitan Airways on 3 June 1985. In addition to their Glasgow–
Bristol, Cardiff and Newcastle services, Metropolitan stepped in to take over the Dan Air Leeds–Bradford
service after they closed their Glasgow station. Metropolitan ceased operations on 31 August 1985.
(John Martindale)

The BAE 748, nicknamed 'Budgies', served a number of the Highlands and Islands routes, particularly
serving the oil industry. This aircraft, G-BGJV, was later sold to Helitours. It was then leased to the Sri
Lankan AF and ended its flying days on approach to Palay AFB, Sri Lanka, where it was shot down on
29 April 1995. (Dr Alastair T. Gardiner)

losing £6 million a year (up from £4 million), which was not sustainable. Senior Icelandair Captain Johannes Snorrason made his last flight from Glasgow on 7 November 1980 on board Boeing 727 TF-FIE some thirty-five years after his first visit to Scotland when he arrived at Largs Bay in a Catalina. Apart from a few British Airways and Loganair pilots he held the record for the most landings and take-offs at Glasgow, certainly the most by a foreign pilot.

Fred Olsen Lockheed Electras operated SAS flight No.SK057 on Wednesdays from 3 December 1980 which routed Stockholm–Glasgow–Manchester–Stockholm.

On 1 May 1980, the airport received a visit from the then world's largest aircraft when a USAF C5A Lockheed Galaxy 69019 arrived to unload a 100-ton mini rescue submarine. This was followed by another visit on 13 May 1980 of another Galaxy (69008) on its way from Rhein Main Air Base at Frankfurt to Dover Air Base in Delaware.

Yugoslav airline JAT Boeing 707 YU-AGJ paid its first visit on 18 May 1980, although JAT's IT flights to the Yugoslavian resorts for the summer season of 1980 were generally undertaken by their DC9s. Aeroflot were also frequent visitors that summer, using TU134s and TU154s.

On 17 June 1980 CASA 212 TR0206 passed through on a delivery flight to the Venezuelan Navy, one of many delivered through Glasgow from the late '70s for the next twenty years or so for the USA and various other military air arms (army, naval and air force) in South and Central America, including Panama, Chile, Paraguay, Colombia, Mexico, Uruguay, Ecuador, Surinam, Dominican Republic and Nicaragua. CASA had pretty much wrapped up the market for this type of aircraft in that part of the world.

There were visits from no less than five RAF VC10s (XV102/3 and XR808/9/10) on 13/14 September 1980. One rare visitor near the year end of 1980 was EL AL Boeing 747 4X-AXB which arrived to take the Scottish National Orchestra to a music festival in Tel Aviv on 26 December.

The passenger figures for 1981/82 showed a further drop of 1.3 per cent on the previous year to 2,296,138. 60 per cent of Glasgow's traffic was domestic and this was down 11 per cent due to a sluggish recovery of business traffic and an above average cancellation rate. European scheduled traffic was down by 8 per cent although European charter flights rose by 27 per cent. Inclusive Tour holiday operations continued to be the major growth area with twenty-two airlines offering flights to fifty destinations. Britannia Airways and Dan Air were the principal operators of the UK airlines with Monarch Airlines Boeing 737s and Boeing 720s also present for the 1982 summer season.

The air transport movement figures declined by 1.2 per cent to 50,700. Glasgow was, however, the only Scottish airport to show an increase in cargo handled (12,700 tons).

Following on from the noise monitoring programme conducted in 1979, a special meeting was held in April 1981 for the purposes of explaining the legal and technical issues involved with regard to aircraft noise problems raised by residents who lived close to the flight path. These residents petitioned for the night closure of the airport. However, the meeting was useful in clearing up a number of misunderstandings about the situation. At the meeting it was apparent that the majority of interested parties were in favour of the benefits of a twenty-four-hour opening of the airport. Assurances were given that noise abatement procedures were being carried out within safety limits by the airlines concerned.

In 1981 Icelandair pulled out of the Glasgow–Copenhagen service after nearly thirty years on the route, followed later in the year by BA who had also operated a direct service. However, after BA had dropped the route, they (Icelandair) had a change of heart and reinstated the route Keflavik–Glasgow–Copenhagen on Monday, Wednesday and Friday, with Boeing 727s operating Mondays and Fridays and a DC8 on Wednesdays. Olympic Airways operated a Glasgow–Corfu service with Boeing 707s during the summer of 1981 on behalf of Budget Holidays. Air Europe also started its first charters from Glasgow in the winter of 1981/82 with IT flights to Geneva. Another charter airline newcomer was Orion Airways which first visited with Boeing 737 G-BGTY on 16 March 1981.

On 11 October 1981 British Airways Concorde G-BOAG arrived for the first time. It was the first time the aircraft had carried fare-paying passengers on a domestic route. Considering

Loganair Fokker F27 Friendship G-IOMA. Built in 1958, she first flew with Aer Lingus as EI-AKB, and made her first visit to Abbotsinch on 2 May 1983 with Manx Airlines. (Gerry McLaughlin)

Hs 748 EI-BSF – one of Ryanair's first aircraft undergoing maintenance in the BA hangar during 20-23 August 1986. (Gerry McLaughlin)

the sensitive issue of aircraft noise during this period not one complaint was received about Concorde's first visit.

The major event of 1982 was the start of the British Midland Airways shuttle service to Heathrow. British Midland had won their appeal (after being refused permission in December 1981) and their new service was launched on 25 October 1982 in direct competition with British Airways.

Douglas DC9-15 G-BMAB flew the first service to Heathrow with Flight No.BD001. There were six return flights per week day in each direction all operated by DC9s, with back up aircraft provided initially by a Monarch Airlines Boeing 737 and a Britannia Airways Boeing 737. At peak periods British Midland briefly used their Boeing 707s instead of their DC9s.

At this point approximately 750,000 passengers flew on the route yearly and early indications showed that once the British Midland service was established they had captured a 28 per cent share of the traffic by the year end. This new service was also reflected in the 7 per cent growth in air transport movements for the year. Having withdrawn free refreshments on the service in August 1980, BA now found themselves having to come up with new marketing initiatives to win passengers. One of these was the so called 'Breakfast Battle', with both airlines offering free breakfasts on morning services to woo passengers. Another BA response to the competition was to select Glasgow as one of the first airports in the UK to be used by the Boeing 757. Services with the Boeing 757 commenced on the shuttle route to Heathrow on 8 February 1983 with G-BIKB.

Passenger traffic overall grew by 5 per cent to just over 2.4 million in the 1982/83 financial year, although, as always, this hid other more drastic movements in the breakdown. Although domestic traffic, which accounted for 58 per cent of the total, increased by 2 per cent, within this figure there was a large 28 per cent drop in domestic charter traffic following the completion of the Sullom Voe Terminal. Domestic scheduled movements rose by 7 per cent, helped by the new British Midland Heathrow service, as previously mentioned, although part of this increase was also due to a recovery of traffic lost to the ATC dispute of the previous year.

For the first time the Airport Consultative Committee broke with the tradition of endorsing the status quo regarding Prestwick by stating that they believed the Government policy of not allowing airlines to fly long-haul flights out of Glasgow was detrimental to potential passengers and less than helpful to Scotland in general. Prior to this, a report published by the House of Commons Scottish Affairs Committee, which looked at proposals to give Prestwick 'freeport' status, again confirmed the existing Lowlands Airport Policy. In its representations to the Select Committee the BAA had strongly rejected the suggestion that there should be a Scottish Airports Authority under the Secretary of State for Scotland, and refuted the implication in the report that the interests of Scottish airports would be better served by a separate airport authority in Scotland. They stated that the current Scottish Airports Division of BAA already had a high degree of autonomy. The formal Government response to the Select Committee's report was a reaffirmation of Prestwick's role as Scotland's intercontinental gateway. However, the Government examined the possibility of 'Stopover Flights'. This was at least a partial recognition of the fact that passengers wanted to fly to both Edinburgh and Abbotsinch by air without having to travel to and from Prestwick. The problem was that the extension of flights to and from Abbotsinch and Edinburgh meant that the existing air service agreements between the USA and Canada would require amendments to enable Prestwick to be the first airport of arrival or last airport of departure. Whilst this had no great impact on services it was a step in the right direction.

Apart from the start of the British Midland Shuttle, there were a few other items of interest happening in 1982. SAS suspended their Glasgow–Copenhagen freight service in February 1982 due to a combination of the runway closure at Glasgow and a lack of aircraft to operate the service. SAS did, however, object to a Finnair application for a Helsinki–Copenhagen–Glasgow–Manchester freight service. BA withdrew Viscounts from the Highlands and Islands services in May 1982 and replaced them with an all Hs748 fleet.

A Britannia Airways Boeing 737 G-OSLA had to return to Glasgow after take-off on 20 April after reporting a major hydraulic failure. The aircraft blocked the runway for several hours as the brakes had seized. The last BA Scottish network Viscount Service was flown by G-AOYM on 8 May 1982 as BA5721 Sumburgh–Kirkwall–Inverness–Glasgow. Embraer Bandeirante G-RLAY flew the first of a new daily Manx Airlines service on 1 November 1982, which was also operated with Short 360s.

Since the BAA takeover, despite a number of years of the airport recording a financial loss, there was a substantial improvement by the end of the 1983/84 financial year, with a recorded £2.5 million trading profit. There was a 2.8 per cent increase in passenger numbers to 2.47 million with the first full year of the new British Midland Heathrow shuttle service achieving a growth of 11 per cent – twice that of all scheduled domestic traffic (up 5.2 per cent). There was a further reduction in domestic charter traffic associated with the run down of construction

Three BAC Concordes, G-BOAA, 'OAB and 'OAD, visiting on 30 August 1983, the day British Airways launched the start of its Heathrow Super Shuttle Service. (Scotsman Publications Archives)

projects in the Shetlands. There was modest growth in outbound charter holiday traffic. Both air transport movements and cargo figures were up on the previous year (by 2.6 per cent and 9.7 per cent respectively). The trend towards increased frequencies on domestic routes led to a 10 per cent increase in scheduled movements.

Among terminal developments during the year was the completion and opening of a centralised search area for domestic passengers on 1 May 1983, which consolidated four separate search areas into one central unit. Other work included the re-siting of the information desk, airline ticket desks and tour operator's desks so as to permit the extension and redevelopment of landside shops. A new short-term car park was constructed in front of the terminal and the first phase of a major landscaping project was begun.

On the airside, trial resurfacing work took place on two stands and fixed ground power units were installed on the domestic pier with the system going into operation during autumn 1983. Work was started on the widening of the main taxiway, at a cost of £1.73 million, to meet the increased usage by larger jet aircraft. The new taxiway was widened from eighteen metres to twenty-three metres to handle Boeing 747s.

The continuing growth in international charter traffic encouraged airlines to introduce larger/wide-bodied aircraft, such as BCAL's DC10, on its Inclusive Tour flights to Palma and Ibiza. BCAL DC10 G-BJZE made the first visit by one of BCAL's DC10s on 23 March 1983 for ground handling trials in preparation for the summer season. British Airways introduced the Boeing 757 on its holiday flights to Athens. Both aircraft generated good load factors but their capacity (360 and 200 passengers respectively) placed a strain on international facilities. For the summer 1984 season BCAL repeated their DC10 programme. British Airways increased the use of their Boeing 757s and Aviaco introduced Boeing 747s and A300 Airbuses on their charter flights to the Spanish mainland, Canary and Balearic Islands. These charters were augmented by the Orion, Monarch and Britannia Airways fleets of Boeing 737s. The larger aircraft capacity on the Inclusive Tour routes in 1983/84 resulted in 4.6 per cent more passengers being carried in 4 per cent fewer aircraft.

On the operational side there was a re-scheduling and re-equipping of some cargo flights after midnight in order to minimize noise disturbance to local residents. The 30 August 1983 saw three BA Concordes (G-BOAA, OAB and OAD) at the airport at the same time for the launch of BA's 'super shuttle' service from Heathrow. The super shuttle was BA's response to the challenge from British Midland's Heathrow shuttle service which, as previously stated, British Midland claimed had captured a 28 per cent share of the traffic as well as generating growth on the route.

Air Ecosse was granted unlimited capacity on the Glasgow–Aberdeen route and introduced the Short 360 to partly replace the Bandeirante being used on the service (which included Belfast). Air Ecosse also started a new Glasgow–Liverpool service in February 1983. BA faced competition from Loganair on the Glasgow–Belfast route with Loganair operating their service into Belfast Harbour Airport (from 7 February 1983), just a short distance from the city centre, whereas the BA service was to Aldergrove airport which was considerably further from the city. Loganair received approval from Western Isles Council to replace their Islanders on the service to Barra with the DHC6 Twin Otter.

An unusual replacement for the usual Hs748 on the Glasgow–Benbecula service on 1 October 1983 was Trident 2 G-AVFN which flew the service via Stornoway due to the delayed arrival of the Hs748.

BA Boeing 747 G-BDXG was diverted to Glasgow from Heathrow on 23 October 1983. This was the fourth time in just over three years that this particular aircraft had been diverted from Heathrow to Glasgow, operating flights from as far afield as Los Angeles and Nairobi.

KLM withdrew its DC9s on the Amsterdam route in March 1983 and replaced them with NLM Fokker F28s. However, the service reverted to DC9s again in November 1983. Air Atlantique won a mail contract to operate between Glasgow and Luton starting on 31 October 1983 using Douglas DC3 G-AMPO.

The highlight of 1983 came on 7 July when the NASA Boeing 747 N905NA, carrying the Space Shuttle, carried out a low pass over the airfield on its way back to the USA after appearing at the Paris Air Show and making a stop at Stansted.

In December 1983 the Civil Aviation Authority granted BMA (British Midland Airways) a licence to operate transatlantic flights directly from Abbotsinch. The BAA appealed against the

Burnthills Bell 206 G-BAKT in April 1985. The Highland helicopter service operated the longest scheduled helicopter service in the world, serving Lochgilphead, Fort William and Glasgow. The service was subsidised by the Highlands and Islands Development Board. (Gerry McLaughlin)

Finnair Douglas DC 9-15 OH-LYE on a very wet-looking apron, operating a Kar-Air flight. Kar-Air operated charter flights on behalf of Finnair during the 1960s and '70s in return for Finnair taking over Kar-Air's domestic routes. OH-LYE visited Glasgow twice (15 June 1975 and 23 August 1979) operating for Kar-Air. (Hugh Brown)

decision on the grounds that it was contrary to Government policy, had significant cost impli- cations for the authority and there was no guarantee that BMA would continue to operate such a service, particularly if a direct Manchester–New York service was started. BAA also stated that whilst they would be happy to accept the service via Prestwick they could not accept the air- lines insistence on only using Abbotsinch because the current scheduled operators at Prestwick would also demand a transfer to Abbotsinch, leaving Prestwick with no scheduled traffic and the inevitability of closure, asset write-off and loss of jobs. Additionally, BAA estimated that the transfer of traffic would require an investment of £15 million to develop facilities made redundant at Prestwick, and finally they stated that the possible closure of Prestwick would leave Scotland without a full inter-continental runway unless the runway at Abbotsinch was extended. The Secretary of State upheld the appeal by BAA and announced that a further review of the Scottish Lowlands Airports Policy would take place. The reality was that the granting of a licence to BMA for the route would end Prestwick's status as the sole long-haul airport for Scotland. Another statement confirming the roles of the three airports was issued with the proviso that if a change had not come about in Prestwick's fortunes by 1989 then the current policy would be reviewed.

Snow and icy conditions during January 1984 were the worst experienced at Glasgow since the airport opened in 1966. Apart from two days during the period 12–26 January it snowed every day putting a great strain on equipment and staff. The airport was shut on twelve occa- sions with a total closure time of nineteen hours and thirty-seven minutes. This period included a closure of five hours for essential runway lighting work, completed during atrocious condi- tions by the airport's electrical department.

The airport facilities had come under severe strain during the summer of 1984 and planning was started on a redevelopment programme to upgrade the airport. Other smaller projects were put in place to improve the facilities including the opening of a more prominent infor- mation desk, the refurbishing of the domestic satellite (formerly known as the Airbus Lounge) and other gaterooms for British Airways, British Midland and British Caledonian. The BA facility was opened on 10 December 1984 to handle all UK flights. A start was also made on the expansion of the outbound luggage sort area.

Another project was the refurbishment of the control tower costing £1.3 million. This included re-equipping the control room and renovating and refurbishing the building both internally and externally. A new motor transport section was provided along with new offices and a boiler room. The newly refurbished control tower was formally opened by the Lord Provost on 24 September 1985.

The airport experienced strong traffic growth in 1984/85 with an increase of 12.8 per cent in total passengers handled to 2.8 million. Cargo was also up by 23 per cent to 15,600 tons. It was the most dramatic annual growth since the exceptional year of 1979/80. This was reflected in an increase of nearly 20 per cent in commercial income to £6.2 million. The increase in passenger figures came equally from Glasgow's two major traffic sectors, scheduled domestic traffic and international charter passengers, which was 22 per cent higher than in 1983/84. There was a recovery in traffic on European scheduled routes with a 6 per cent increase. A larger increase in average passenger loads was due to the increasing use of larger aircraft on international charters.

A Parliamentary question tabled by Richard Page MP to the Transport Secretary asked how many passengers from the major UK regional airports had flown to and from the two main London airports in 1984 and what percentage had transferred to international flights. The figures for Glasgow were:

Glasgow–Heathrow 940,000 (26 per cent)
Glasgow–Gatwick 132,000 (25 per cent)

The percentage of passengers transferring to international flights was the lowest out of the regional airports with the exception of Aberdeen.

On the first anniversary (30 August 1984) of the launch of their Super Shuttle Service, British Airways claimed to be carrying eight out of ten of all passengers on the Shuttle routes out of Heathrow (Glasgow, Belfast and Edinburgh) despite offering only six in ten of the flights and seven in ten of the seats available. In all BA claimed to have carried a total of over 2.5 million passengers across the three routes with Heathrow–Glasgow remaining the busiest. Whatever the statistics were, the competition between the airlines ensured that the winners were the passengers and Glasgow Airport.

Out on the airfield the widening of the main taxiway was finished in May 1984 and was used by an Iberia Boeing 747 for operations the day after it opened. Air Ecosse suspended their Glasgow–Belfast and Glasgow–Dublin services and closed their Glasgow office in November 1984. They were still operating a single Glasgow–Aberdeen return flight using a leased Peregrine Air Services Jetstream 31 and were awarded the former Genair route to Teeside and Hull which was operated by Casair Cessna 404. Air Ecosse also applied to operate a Glasgow–Hamburg route in November 1984.

Canafrica DC 8-61 EC-DYY on 9 June 1986. This DC 8 flew for a number of owners after CTA, then went into storage at Dallas Love Field. In May 2009 it was languishing at Opa Locka, Florida. (John Allan)

Air UK started a Glasgow–Southampton service using an Air Ecosse Bandeirante from 3 January 1984, but this was suspended by October of that year. There were a number of changes to the airlines at Glasgow in 1984. Genair collapsed and Air Ecosse faced difficulties with their routes contracting, although this was offset by Metropolitan Airways and Air UK taking over some of the routes. Genair (which had been part of the BCAL commuter group) went into receivership on 13 July 1984 with the last Genair service into Glasgow arriving that day (Short 330 G-BKDO on flight No.EN107/8). Air UK took over from British Caledonian on the Glasgow–Newcastle–Amsterdam route using BIA's (British Island Airways) BAe1-11 G-AXBB. At the time Air UK was the largest foreign operator out of Amsterdam. Dan Air also withdrew from Glasgow Airport due to a reduction in domestic charter requirements for the Shetlands oil industry. The Dan Air Glasgow–Leeds–Cardiff–Bristol route which they had operated with the Hs748 since 1976 was transferred to Metropolitan Airways in September 1984. Metropolitan operated the route with the Short 330 until September 1985. Cargo carrier Air Bridge took over the Swissair cargo service on from 26 March 1984 with their Vanguard/'Merchantman'. DC9 HB-IFW operated the last Swissair cargo service on 23 March 1984, a service this aircraft had operated for ten years.

Manx Airlines introduced two Short 360s (G-ISLE and G-LEGS) on their Isle of Man service in spring 1984. On 5 June 1984 a Dan Air BAe1-11 G-TARO arrived which was the first visit of a ROMBAC1-11. These were 1-11s built under licence in Romania.

RAF VC10s continued to visit Glasgow on a regular basis, with six visits being made by five aircraft between 16 and 18 July 1984, XV106 coming in on 16 and 17 July. Two new BA Hs748s (G-HDBA and G-HDBB) arrived on 13/14 December 1984 to join G-BCOE/COF. Earlier that year, in April, BA had entered into an agreement with Britoil to block 12,000 seats a year (ten per sector) on the Glasgow–Aberdeen route.

On the charter side, the range of aircraft types through the airport increased with Iberia scheduling Boeing 747 and A-310 Airbus services to Spanish resorts, joining British Caledonian DC10s on the Palma route. Palma itself continued to be the most popular route from Glasgow with 202,200 passengers in 1984/85. The Tenerife route showed substantial growth of 49 per cent. Iberia's weekly 747 service augmented by Monarch's and British Airway's Boeing 757 flights helped to contribute to this growth.

Scottish Executive Airways applied to operate Glasgow–Brussels/Frankfurt and ordered two SF340s for delivery in June 1985. They also bought the defunct Aerotime but were unable to use their (Aerotime's) routes.

The main project of 1985 was the resurfacing of the runway at a cost of £3.5 million. The runway was closed five nights a week from 14 April to 18 October 1985 from 21.45 to 05.45. Unfortunately this resulted in the temporary loss of cargo and mail traffic which took some time to rebuild.

The terminal facilities came under pressure in the summer of 1985, particularly at weekends. To improve the situation, work was started on an interim development to the international facilities in autumn 1985. This included an extension to the departures lounge, a new duty/tax free shop plus the completion of two new gateroom catering facilities and the refurbishment of the bar in the international departures lounge, at a total cost of £2 million. Due to the congestion being experienced, a major review was undertaken during 1985 culminating in a decision by the Board of Directors in November of that year to expand the international facilities westwards from the terminal building.

Another improvement was the opening of the new airport fire station in December 1985, while the BAA's first Javelin MkII fire appliance became operational on the same day as the opening of the station.

Birmingham Executive Airways, which was operating a service to Birmingham, replaced the Jetstream 31 on the route with a Saab 340 on 19 February 1985.

On the scheduled movements side Air UK had considered buying two Fokker F28s on their Amsterdam route but eventually used leased BIA BAe1-11s in 1985.

Malinair Dornier Do228-201 G-MLNR on 17 June 1987. Malinair had a relatively short life of less than two and a half years. The Swiss Falcon 50 in the background is HB-IAE. (Dr Alastair T. Gardiner)

Malinair was formed in June 1985 by Glasgow lawyer Frank Cannon, with Duncan MacIntosh (ex-Loganair) as chairman, starting a scheduled service to Donegal from Glasgow in early 1986 using a BN Islander. The airline expanded almost immediately but some felt the expansion was too quick.

Three other new airlines also started services. The first was Air Luton which took over the Air Atlantique Glasgow–Luton postal contract in February 1985 using DC3s. The second was Air Stansted which started a Glasgow–Stansted service with Bandeirantes and later Short 330s. The third new operator was Aerotime which later changed its name to Scottish Executive Airways. They applied for Glasgow–Brussels and Frankfurt routes and placed an order for two Saab 340s for delivery in June 1985.

KLM closed their Glasgow station in autumn 1985 with Servisair taking over the handling for the airline. Loganair had been busy in 1985 evaluating the SF340, Dornier Do228 and the Dash 8, and applied for new Glasgow–Brussels/ Manchester/ Cologne routes as well as taking out options on two ATPs for delivery in 1987. BAF (British Air Ferries) took over the newspaper run from Air Bridge Carriers on 11 December 1985, flying Viscounts to Southend.

On the Inclusive Tour side, holidaymakers flying from Glasgow switched their traditional allegiance away from Spain in 1985 to include destinations in Greece, Yugoslavia, Portugal and Cyprus, which were all gaining in popularity. Several new destinations were served for the first time, including Paphos, several Greek Island airports, more Spanish resorts and several European cities. Airtours started charter operations from Glasgow and Britannia used Boeing 767s on their services for the first time.

A couple of new scheduled routes came into operation. SAS expanded their destinations from Glasgow to include Stavanger and Copenhagen, Lufthansa started a service to Dusseldorf on 1 April 1986, and British Airways added a mid-morning flight to their Heathrow shuttle service.

On the downside the year saw the demise of Metropolitan Airways on 31 August 1985, although a licence to operate similar inter-regional airways routes was awarded to Brown Air Services. Metropolitan Airways had been operating from Glasgow to Bristol, Cardiff, Leeds/ Bradford and Newcastle. Brown Air Services initially took over the old Dan Air Glasgow–Leeds/Bradford route using a Grumman Gulfstream 1. They later rebranded themselves as Capital Airways in October 1987.

SAS DC 9-21 OY-KGE in September 1987. The route to Copenhagen has had mixed fortunes over the years with a number of airlines flying the route from Glasgow, some with more success than others. (Dr Alastair T. Gardiner)

An unusual visitor passing through on 12 January 1985 was CV240 N314H belonging to Air Rajneesh, the 'airline' of the Indian 'sex guru' Baghwan Shree Rajneesh. Other visitors of note in 1985 included the first visit by a Boeing 747SP (SP meaning Special Performance), A6-AMR, belonging to the Government of the United Arab Emirates, on 27 June. The first visit of a Lockheed Tristar-500, CS-TEB, which flew the service normally covered by a TAP Boeing 707, occurred on 28 July. The 29 December 1985 was close to the end of the year but also signalled the end of an era at Glasgow when Trident 3 G-AWZO made the last shuttle flight by a Trident. All the BA shuttle services were now operated by the Boeing 757.

After only eleven months of operating the Glasgow–Luton postal contract, Air Luton went into liquidation in February 1986 and the contract was taken over by Topflight using Air Luton's DC3s. By March 1986 three airlines were operating newspaper flights. The pattern of flights had been altered with News International starting operations with their Kinning park presses in January 1986. British Air Ferries flew Glasgow–Belfast, Southend–Glasgow and Glasgow–Dublin with Viscounts. Aer Lingus Boeing 737 freighters flew two weekend flights from Glasgow to Dublin and Loganair flew Glasgow–Liverpool and Edinburgh–Glasgow with Short 360s.

In the summer of 1986 Malinair started operating the Aberdeen–Glasgow–Belfast service which had previously been operated by the now defunct Air Ecosse. A Dornier 228 leased from Schreiner Airways (PH-DSO, re-registered G-MLDO) was operated using Air Ecosse's route licence and WG flight code. Malinair already employed BN Islanders G-MALI and G-MALN on the Glasgow–Carrickfinn route (started in January 1986) and for night mail work. Amongst other routes, Malinair applied to operate new Glasgow–Dundee and Glasgow–Sligo services.

Whilst Malinair was expanding at this time, poor loads on the Glasgow–Amsterdam route forced Air UK to downgrade the Bae1-11 used on the route to an F27 Friendship. The transit stop at Leeds/Bradford was dropped and an F27 was also put on this route at the same time. The drop in numbers on these routes was believed to be related to the decline in the North Sea oil industry. During September/October 1986 the Amsterdam route was served, as per the summer schedule, by a Convair 580 leased from Partnair whilst the Bae1-11 was withdrawn for a major overhaul.

Britannia Airways had mixed fortunes in the summer 1986 season. Using leased aircraft they experienced a number of mechanical problems with various aircraft and a few serious delays, one Tenerife flight arriving back at Glasgow twenty-seven hours late. Their leased Spantax DC8 EC-DYY finished the end of its lease on 31 August 1986 with a spectacular high speed approach and go around. Air Ecosse ceased operations in 1986 and were formally wound up on 19 January 1987.

BA reintroduced their Glasgow–Dusseldorf/Munich services, both going via Birmingham, in 1986. They did, however, face competition from DLT operating on behalf of Lufthansa which started a new Glasgow–Dusseldorf service on 1 April 1986 using Embraer 120 Brasilias. The first service was flown with PT-SIH. A new SAS service Glasgow–Aberdeen–Bergen started in April 1986 was altered in autumn 1987 to run Oslo–Stavanger–Aberdeen–Glasgow–Copenhagen.

BCAL ran down its engineering base in 1986. Started in 1967 by BUA with a staff of one station engineer, four engineers, four fitters and eight maintenance workers. The base looked after night stopping Gatwick aircraft and the Newcastle/Amsterdam aircraft, also dealing with any problems which arose on other BCAL flights.

New developments included the addition of eight new aircraft parking stands 27–34 (plus one for general aviation – 35) and design work for a new coach station at the foot of the international pier was started. The stands on the new apron area were opened in November 1987.

Icelandair operated a Reykjavik–Vagar (Faroes)–Glasgow service through the winter schedule of 1987/88 using F27s on Mondays and Tuesdays. From mid-December 1987 the Boeing 727 Reykjavik service operated through Glasgow from Gothenburg–Copenhagen.

Malinair started a Glasgow–Teeside–Gatwick service using a Dornier 228. Additionally, Malinair operated a BN2 Islander from Glasgow to Humberside.

Despite its promising beginnings with their stated aim of becoming a large Dornier 228 operator, Malinair ceased operating on 19 June 1987. The two Malinair Do228s were impounded at Glasgow and Aberdeen owing £35,000 in unpaid landing fees. They were taken over by a reformed Air Ecosse which started operating again on 1 July 1987. Air Ecosse had been in administration since January until they were bought by Traditional Investments for £477,000. Another airline having problems was Chieftain Airways. Their two Hs748s (G-GLAS and G-EDIN) had arrived at Glasgow to start new services on 29 March 1987 but they had ceased operations six weeks later on 13 May following a winding up petition. New financial backing was sought but not forthcoming.

After the takeover of British Caledonian by British Airways in December 1987, the CAA granted a licence to operate the Glasgow–Gatwick route to Air UK in 1988. They placed an

MEA (Middle East Airlines) Boeing 707-3B4C OD-AFD on 25 June 1989 operating on behalf of Paramount Airways. (Dr Alistair T. Gardiner)

order for BAe 146–300s to operate a high frequency service (up to seven return flights a day) on both Gatwick–Glasgow and Gatwick–Edinburgh services from the start of the winter 1988/89 timetable. The 112-seat aircraft offered a 22 per cent increase in capacity over the British Caledonian BAC1-11s previously used on the route.

There were ups and downs on the Spanish IT side during the summer season of 1987: Spantax dropped from twelve to four flights a week and Aviaco were down from thirteen to three flights a week. Air Europa started for the first time with four flights a week and Hispania increased from one to seven a week.

Air Bridge Carriers had some recompense for losing their night freight contract back to Swissair when they gained a new freight contract for Glasgow–East Midlands–Amsterdam. Swissair took over from Air Bridge with their A-310-200 and A-310-300 aircraft replacing the Air Bridge 'Merchantman'. A-310 HP-IPH flew the first service on 2 November 1987.

Tragedy struck on 4 June 1987 when a Beech Bonanza N6757Y crashed one mile southwest of Howwood, six miles from the airport. Sadly, both occupants were killed instantly.

In June 1988 the BAA Board approved an investment of £47 million to refurbish the terminal building (increasing its size by 70 per cent) and surrounding areas to meet demand up to the mid-1990s. 1988/89 saw a weak holiday sector which showed a small percentage decline, but this was offset by a strong performance on scheduled domestic and European services which led to an increase in overall passenger numbers of 7.8 per cent. An increase in services resulted in steep growth of 11 per cent on services to London. Air UK began services to Gatwick and Stansted and both British Airways and British Midland increased the frequency of their Heathrow services. International operations showed limited growth and, as already stated, the summer Inclusive Tour traffic was disappointing, although the winter 1988 Inclusive Tour figures showed real growth for the first time.

There was a large increase (33 per cent) in cargo handled when the figure for 1988/89 increased to 15,281 metric tons.

On the European airlines scheduled services there were a few changes in 1988. Air France started a welcome new service on 26 March 1988 to Paris (Charles De Gaulle), operating six days a week from Aberdeen. KLM decided to hand over their dedicated service to Air UK in March 1988. The last dedicated KLM flight with KLM aircraft was on 23 February 1988 with Boeing 737 PH-BDK and the last DC9 (PH-DNP) on 2 February 1988. Until the Air UK takeover KLM leased a Transavia Boeing 737 in full KLM colours, making their last flight on 25 March 1988.

Nationair DC 8-61 C-GMXQ. Nationair collapsed in May 1993 with severe financial difficulties. C-GMXQ crashed at Jeddah on a Haj flight on 11 July 1991, due to under-inflated tyres which overheated and caught fire, with the tragic loss of all on board. (Dr Alastair T. Gardiner)

Aeroflot TU-134 CCCP65815 in front of the control tower. Aeroflot were regular visitors in the 1970s
and '80s, with TU-134s, TU-154s and IL-62s. (Hugh Brown)

An old Glasgow regular, Sabena, started a Glasgow–Manchester–Brussels service on 1 February
1988 with Fokker F28s. However, they decided to alter the routing after only a few months (on
15 May) to Brussels–Edinburgh–Glasgow–Brussels.

After the changes to their schedule in autumn 1987 SAS again decided to alter their schedules in the summer of 1988. They altered the days of their Stavanger and Copenhagen services
and from July added Dublin from Copenhagen via Glasgow for six days of the week.

Icelandair again tinkered with their service in 1988. One of their two Reykjavik–Faroes–
Glasgow services was operated through Egilsstadir and they pulled out of the Copenhagen
route stating poor aircraft utilisation as the reason. Also, on the debit side DLT decided to drop
their Sunday Dusseldorf service in spring 1988 due to a lack of demand.

British Midland had taken delivery of their new BAe ATPs and decided to introduce them
on their route to East Midlands Airport in June 1988.

Barely a year would pass without the issue of an airline being forced into receivership.
In 1988 it was the turn of Spantax with debts of £40 million. This was followed by South East
Air, one of the seemingly countless operators of the various mail and newspaper runs. They
had taken over the former Euroair Glasgow–Luton–Edinburgh mail service the previous year.
Their Herald G-ATIG was impounded at Gatwick.

Scottish European Airways was formed from the shell of the ill fated Chieftain Airways for
flights to Frankfurt, Brussels and Hamburg using Chieftain's two Hs748s (G-GLAS and G-
EDIN) which had been grounded and securely parked since May 1987. The official start date
was 14 November 1988, initially to Frankfurt and Brussels, although charters had already began
the previous month.

Third Level operator Capital Airlines added Bristol to their main route Glasgow–Leeds–
Cardiff on 4 July 1988 on which they were operating a Shorts 360.

In January 1989 the BAA requested a review of the Lowlands Airport Policy, but this was
refused by the Secretary of State for Transport. Instead, the Government announced plans to
improve surface access to Prestwick. However, events were to take a very different turn from a
quite unexpected source. Air 2000 seemed an unlikely candidate to break the deadlock over the
unbending rule that all Scottish long-haul flights had to go to Prestwick. The airline had started
operations in 1987 with two Boeing 757s operating charters from Manchester. It expanded
and the following year based another Boeing 757 at Abbotsinch to operate European charters.
Problems arose when Air 2000 applied to operate charter flights to Orlando in Florida from
Abbotsinch rather than Prestwick. It was probably assumed that a small airline like Air 2000
was of little consequence and could easily be rebuffed. The airline was refused the right to fly

direct flights and had to make a technical stop at Prestwick which added considerably to costs. Air 2000 challenged the Traffic Distribution Rules and took the Government to court at the Court of Session in Edinburgh. At the same time United Airlines had lodged an application with the CAA for Glasgow–Washington and Chicago flights, leaving Prestwick out of the application completely. Air 2000 achieved a stunning victory forcing a complete rethink of the Government's policy in relation to the Lowland airports, opening up direct transatlantic flights from Abbotsinch and Edinburgh Airport.

Ryanair started their first Glasgow service (to Dublin) for the summer 1988 season on 27 April 1988 with Bae1-11 EI-BVH undertaking the first flight. Lufthansa upgraded their EMB120 on the Dusseldorf route to ATR42s from spring 1989. Presumably to add some capacity due to DLT dropping their Sunday service the previous year.

Air UK recorded considerable increases on the Gatwick route since taking it over from BCAL the previous year. Passenger figures for May and June 1989 were up by 51 per cent and 61 per cent from the same months a year previously.

Aer Lingus introduced the Fokker 50 on their service to Glasgow (as well as all the rest of their Dublin to UK provincial airports) at the end of May 1989 and increased the frequency. They also transferred their two Saturday night Boeing 737 freighter services from Prestwick to Abbotsinch.

In spring 1989, having dropped their Keflavik–Glasgow–Copenhagen route, Icelandair applied to fly Keflavik–Glasgow–Frankfurt from November 1989 using fifth freedom rights (the right to carry passengers between third countries outside the country of origin of the airline). They started to replace their long serving Boeing 727s with Boeing 737-400s.

There were a couple of unusual events during 1989. On 3 February a British Airways Boeing 747 was diverted into the airport. The flight had originated in Cairo and was on its way from Heathrow to Toronto. A woman passenger reported that her luggage appeared to have been tampered with before taking off from Cairo. Security staff at Glasgow searched both baggage and aircraft but found nothing suspicious and the aircraft continued on to Toronto. The aircraft had not diverted to the more obvious choice of Prestwick due to crosswinds there. Another unusual event at the airport was the sight of Gill Air's Short 330 G-BPMA lying on its back on 13 February after having been blown over by severe gales. The aircraft was a write-off.

Air 2000 Boeing 757 G-OOOH. Air 2000 finally forced the Government to back down over their insistence of Prestwick as Scotland's long-haul gateway. (Dr Alastair T. Gardiner)

1990–2000 – Direct Transatlantic Flights and Expansion

After years of uncertainty following the successful legal challenge by Air 2000, the major event of the year 1990 was the decision by the Secretary of State for Transport to change the Scottish Lowland Airports Policy. The announcement was made by Cecil Parkinson on 6 March 1990. Subject to international air agreements the new 'Open Skies' policy allowed airlines to fly services to whichever of the three Lowland airports (Prestwick, Abbotsinch or Edinburgh) best suited the passenger market from May 1990.

The new policy brought immediate changes to Abbotsinch. The carriers at Prestwick serving North America (Northwest Airlines and Air Canada) now transferred their flights from Prestwick to Abbotsinch. Air Canada moved their operations from Prestwick to Abbotsinch on 16 May, although their freight service continued to use Prestwick for the time being. The first direct transatlantic flight occurred on 2 May 1990 with Northwest Airlines flying in from Boston at 08.04 with Douglas DC10 N149US. The service was daily, although it was reduced to Monday/Wednesday/Friday/Sunday for the winter schedule.

United Airlines dropped their initial plan to operate an immediate transatlantic service out of Abbotsinch, instead concentrating on a new Manchester–Washington service first.

Two airlines which had expressed initial interest in operating a service to New York JFK were British Midland and Virgin, but they withdrew their applications early in 1990. The transfer of services was soon followed by new routes to Chicago by American Airlines from 16 May using Boeing 767s and New York with British Airways who were granted permission to fly to New York JFK from Glasgow marking their return to Scottish transatlantic flights after a gap of eight years. They intended to start with three flights a week in 1991 using Lockheed Tristars. Although not a scheduled operator American Transat operated charter flights from Glasgow to New York for the 1990 summer season.

The other side of the coin was, of course, a large decrease in traffic at Prestwick, with the airport returning to making a financial loss.

Over on the European side Sabena introduced the BAe 146-200 in May on their Brussels service with an extra daily Fokker F28 service planned for a January 1991 start.

There was also activity on the domestic front with new routes being opened in 1990 by Brymon Airways to Bristol and Manx Airlines to Cardiff via Liverpool which started on 11 June 1990 using Short 360s. There had been a great deal of interest in serving Cardiff in 1990, not

BA Lockheed L1011-385-1 Tristar 200 G-BHBR. BA used Tristars on their New York service in 1990 and 1991, before using smaller-capacity aircraft like the Boeing 767 and 757. (Dr Alastair T. Gardiner)

only from Manx Airlines. Celtic Airways, Inter European Airways and Brymon had all applied to operate on this route. In addition to Manx, Brymon were granted permission to operate a service, which they started in December 1990 using DHC8s.

Monarch Airlines closed its base at Glasgow in 1990 after twelve years. They had flown eighteen weekly flights in the summer of 1989. However, most of its Glasgow work was with Owners Abroad which was now using Air 2000 (its own airline). Most of the Monarch staff were relocated to Luton and Manchester. Air UK introduced a fourth Glasgow–Amsterdam daily service departing at 06.30 and Dan Air operated a new charter flight to Perpignan on Saturdays using Bae1-11s.

There were no less than five airlines using Glasgow which ceased operations in 1990. The first, British Island Airways, went into receivership on 1 February and grounded its six Bae1-11s and four MD83s. The next was Odyssey International which ceased operating on 27 April with their contracts and some of their aircraft being taken over by Nationair.

On the same date Scottish European, which had had a promising beginning and was planning to extend its routes from Glasgow to include Nice, Milan (Linate) and Barcelona, went into receivership and their aircraft were impounded at Frankfurt and Manchester. The next airline to be affected was Crown Air which had planned a Glasgow–Vancouver service but ceased operations almost immediately. The fifth was Capital Airlines which had started a Glasgow–Jersey Saturday summer charter service using BAe146s but suspended operations on 28 June with a projected loss of £6 million. They had already lost £3 million in 1989. Loganair took over the Capital Airlines Glasgow–Leeds/Bradford service. Loganair, which appeared to go from strength to strength, introduced the Bae146 on their Glasgow–Manchester service early in 1990. Despite the failure of these airlines there appeared to be no shortage of new start ups. Southern Airlines, a new start up in 1990, applied to operate a Glasgow–Bournemouth service.

On 28 December 1990 a USAF C-5 Galaxy 50010 made an emergency landing whilst en route from Rhein-Main Air Base at Frankfurt on its way to Dover AFB in Delaware, USA. The aircraft had developed a hydraulic problem but landed safely and was attended by two further C-5Bs (70029 and 60011) along with a Lockheed C-141 Starlifter 70018. It departed for RAF Mildenhall on 31 December 1990.

A £1 million supplementary check-in facility was opened to cope with the increase in passenger numbers and work continued throughout 1990 on the £55 million terminal development programme with some of the areas being opened in October 1990. Stage two of the projected redevelopment was reassessed to take account of the increase in transatlantic traffic. There was strong growth in scheduled domestic and European services which more than compensated for a weak outbound holiday sector.

The airport took its environmental responsibilities seriously and in 1990 entered into an agreement to protect Paisley Moss which was Strathclyde's first local nature reserve. Paisley Moss fell within the boundary of the airport and contained five plant species which were very rare in the UK and nineteen which were rare in Scotland.

Air Canada announced in March 1991 that there had been a successful increase in business following the move from Prestwick and they increased the Glasgow–Toronto schedule to daily from June 1992 and Glasgow–Halifax was increased to three flights a week. The last Air Canada Lockheed Tristar service into Glasgow was C-GAGH on 27 October 1991. However, there were mixed fortunes for two other transatlantic carriers, American Airlines reduced capacity to Chicago in March 1991 to four flights a week and British Airways delayed the start of its new direct New York service because of reduced passenger numbers caused by the Gulf War and instead used a service originating at Gatwick which flew empty to Glasgow and the same in reverse. The first service was flown by Tristar G-BEAK on 3 August 1990. British Airways then announced the start of a dedicated New York service from 1 November 1991 using Boeing 767s with G-BNWH undertaking the first flight. Britannia Airways operated their first transatlantic service from Glasgow on 1 May 1991 to Orlando (via Bangor, Maine) with Boeing 757 G-OAHI.

On 23 December 1993 United Boeing 767 N609UA skidded off runway 23 at link 5, closing the runway for four hours. The shorter cross runway was de-iced allowing some services to continue operating. (Gerry McLauglin)

During the year Loganair acquired five new Jetstream 31s and applied to operate Glasgow–Southampton. They also ordered three Jetstream 41s for delivery in 1992 and reintroduced ATP services to Manchester from Glasgow after an eighteen-month break.

There was only one major airline casualty (operating out of Glasgow) in 1991 when Air Europe went into liquidation on 8 March. On a more positive note on the charter side, Caledonian Airways set up a third UK base at Glasgow for the summer of 1992 operating tours on behalf of Airtours, Grecian and Cypriana Holidays.

On 24 November 1991 a Northwest DC10, N161US, had to return to the airport after it suffered a birdstrike on take-off for New York JFK. There was damage to the starboard engine and a replacement was flown in on Short Belfast G-BFYU of Heavy Lift Cargo Airlines on 26 November and the DC10 departed on 27 November just after Boeing 747 N605US had arrived to operate the normal service. The previous month had seen some unusual American visitors on the same day (20 October) with United Airlines Boeing 747 N160UA being diverted to take on fuel, and also former US president Ronald Reagan arrived with his wife Nancy on board the *Forbes Business* magazine's Boeing 727 N60FM (named *Capitalist Tool*).

In January 1992 BAA announced plans for the second stage of the development plan intended to raise passenger capacity from 5.5 million to 10 million. This was to include a new international arrival pier able to accommodate up to eight wide-bodied aircraft and new taxiways and aprons. An international departure lounge, baggage arrivals hall and immigration area was to be added with the work expected to be complete by 1996. The first stage work which had already been carried out on the terminal building, expanding it by 70 per cent, was formally opened by Princess Anne on 15 June 1992. Eighteen jobs were lost at the airport at the end of June 1992 when Shell closed its refuelling service, blaming declining sales and profitability.

A most unusual weather event occurred in the early evening of 28 January 1992 when visibility was below Category 1 limits at Abbotsinch, Prestwick and Edinburgh airports, necessitating diversions to Aberdeen, Manchester and Newcastle. It is very rare for all three Scottish airports to be closed at the same time. The three BA Hs748s were withdrawn in the spring of 1992

G-AVMK Bae 1-11-510ED on 10 July 1995. She was leased by Sabena (with G-AVMI) from European Air Charter to operate their service to Brussels in the mid-1990s. (Dr Alastair T. Gardiner)

with the last service (Glasgow–Aberdeen –Stornoway–Inverness) being flown on 27 March by G-BCOE. The three aircraft were sitting idly by the BA engineering hangar by early May. On 25 October BA also changed the New York destination airport from JFK to Newark to allow better links with US Air.

Air Canada introduced Boeing 747s on its four days a week route to Toronto from 25 May 1992. This was upgraded to a daily service from mid-June 1992 whilst the Glasgow–Halifax route stayed at twice weekly with Boeing 767s. The buoyancy in transatlantic traffic was represented by a growth of 26 per cent in passenger numbers over 1991.

There were two changes to airline names during 1992 in relation to Glasgow. The first was Brymon Airways merging with Birmingham European to become Brymon European Airways in the autumn. They started a new Glasgow–Humberside service using Jetstream 31s. The other change took place on 23 October when British Airways absorbed Dan Air.

Both Air Sul and Nortjet ceased operations in February with the Nortjet commitments out of Glasgow met by Air Europa and Futura.

Lufthansa ceased their service to Dusseldorf at the end of March 1992 but started Glasgow–Frankfurt from 1 July using Boeing 737s. Other positive news in 1992 was the start of a new service to Palma in the summer by LTE, making its first appearance at Glasgow operating the service on Friday mornings with Boeing 757s. SAS introduced MD87s in the spring on the Copenhagen service and also re-launched the Glasgow–Stavanger service with Fokker 50s for four days of the week. One of the more unusual diversions was Condor Boeing 767 D-ABUZ on 12 June 1992 which diverted because of a blocked toilet! Rich International operated a series of flights using Tristars during the summer 1992 season on behalf of World Airways.

There was a tragic start to the new year when Titan Airways Embraer Bandeirante G-ZAPE crashed on Ponsonby Fell in Cumbria inbound for Glasgow from Southend on 13 January with the loss of three lives.

A new VIP parking ramp came into operation on 1 May 1993 when Portuguese Air Force Falcon 50, serial 7403, became the first aircraft to use it. Work commenced on the building of the new £40 million international pier. The new pier was planned to have six new wide-

Easyjet Boeing 737-33V G-EZYH on 20 December 1998 displaying the airline's opposition to BA's low-cost airline GO, which was bought in May 2002 by Easyjet for £374 million. (Fred Seggie)

body stands. For the duration of the building work, the domestic baggage reclaim was closed off and removed to a temporary building erected at the previous stand 25 at the root of the domestic pier. The car hire desks were also moved outside the international arrivals area whilst the work was carried out. There was considerable pressure on facilities during this period and there was something of a record on Saturday 10 July 1993 when there were ten wide-bodied aircraft on the ground at the same time.

The cargo facilities were also starting to come under pressure and work costing £2 million started in December 1993. The facilities were then over twenty years old and were struggling to cope. Cargo figures had increased by 12 per cent in the previous year alone. Renfrewshire Enterprise commissioned a study into developing the north side of the airport.

Passenger figures increased by 11.6 per cent to 4.7 million with transatlantic services continuing to show growth. United Airlines started a Glasgow–Washington service on 10 June 1993 with Boeing 767 N608UA, in the process becoming the fifth airline to operate transatlantic flights from Glasgow. An unfortunate incident on 23 December 1993 involved a United Boeing 767 N609A on the Washington service skidding off runway 23 at link 5 and blocking it for nearly four hours.

Another unfortunate occurrence took place on 1 June 1993 when a 5ft x 3ft carbon fibre fairing between the wing and the body fell from a British Airways Boeing 757 and landed in a school sports field at Littlehill Primary School, Glasgow. Fortunately there were no injuries. The 757 was climbing through 7,000ft when the fairing fell away. British Airways introduced the Boeing 767 to their Shuttle services operating one return flight per day from October.

Loganair started a new service to Connaught from 18 June 1993. Air Canada celebrated its fiftieth anniversary of flights to Scotland between Glasgow and Toronto by reducing fares by £50 during June and July 1993 as a special promotion. Lufthansa Cargo started a weekday freight service to Frankfurt on 27 September 1993 using Fokker F27s leased from Amadeus Air. Aer Lingus withdrew their Boeing 737-200s at the end of October 1993 after twenty-four years.

On the debit side SAS announced the suspension of services to Glasgow after twenty-five years with the Stavanger service finishing on 9 January and Copenhagen on 27 February 1993.

Nationair ceased operations in early April with all their summer operations taken over by Caledonian using Boeing 757s and DC10s.

A major development, adding to the airport's capacity, was the opening of the new international pier which opened on 17 November. There was seating for 1,200 passengers. Stands 2–12 were for off-stand parking whilst stands 4–8 were for general aviation movements, adding to the capacity of the general aviation area. There was also a realignment of the stands on the old international pier when three new stands were created on 23 May 1994 by the realignment of stands 5 and 9 and parking aircraft further off the end of the pier. A new security screening system to detect explosives in hold baggage was tested at Glasgow before being introduced to other BAA airports including Heathrow. On the airfield itself the old Hangar 12 was pulled down between 24 May and 21 June.

In 1994 twelve-year-old Vicki Van Meter flew a Cessna 210L (N27S) named *Harmony* from her home in Agusta Maine to Europe via Goose Bay in Greenland and Reykjavik before making a night stop in Glasgow on 7/8 June 1994. She continued her journey to Biggin Hill, Brussels, Frankfurt and Paris. Although accompanied by her Flying Instructor, she flew the plane herself for the duration of her journey. It was a remarkable feat for a twelve year old. Sadly, she died in 2008 at the age of twenty-six in tragic circumstances.

Air Malta introduced its first scheduled flights to Scotland with a new service Glasgow–Malta on 5 May 1994, with Boeing 737-300 9H-ABR operating the first flight.

Air Canada announced St Johns as a new twice-weekly destination from the summer of 1994, with the Boeing 767 going on to Halifax. Set against this good news was the major disappointment of Northwest Airlines announcement that they were suspending their Glasgow–Boston service on 25 October 1994, thus ending a fifteen-year connection with Scotland. The reason was that although there were good load factors in economy class there were not enough business class passengers to make the service viable. This was followed by yet more disappointment when United Airlines announced that they were also pulling out of their Glasgow–Washington service for the same reasons given by Northwest. The last United Airlines flight was undertaken by Boeing 767 N605UA on 31 October 1994.

There was a large reorganisation of Loganair in January 1994. Eight ATPs and three Jetstream 41s were transferred to Manx Airlines (both were within the British Midland Group) leaving only Short 360s. The physical deployment of the aircraft came in March that year and in April Loganair signed a franchise deal with BA after the completion of a buy-out deal which meant that from July 1994 all Loganair aircraft would fly in BA Express colours. Loganair also took over the BA Glasgow to Inverness, Aberdeen and Belfast services. The last operation of a Loganair Jetstream 31 was on 26 March 1994 when G-LOGR arrived from Edinburgh.

There were a number of developments on the operational cargo side in 1994, Channel Express commenced weekday cargo flights in October 1994 to East Midlands Airport on behalf of UPS using Fokker F27 G-JEAE which replaced Titan Airways Short 360. Hunting Cargo's Lockheed Electras replaced European Air Transport's Convair 580s on the DHL contract in April 1994 and British Airways Cargo leased in Arrow Air DC8-63F N345JW to operate Gothenburg–Glasgow–Columbus Ohio three-days-a-week freight schedule. Kalitta took over from Arrow Air on this service with DC8 N813K until the service ceased in March 1995. Finally, the last Viscounts operating on a regular basis from Glasgow since 1966 was in August 1994 when British World Airways moved their newspaper operations from Glasgow to Edinburgh.

There were three visits by BA Concordes towards the end of 1994; G-BOAF on 2 October, G-BOAC on 30 November and G-BOAA on 27 December.

Details for a £27 million rail link to be drawn up by 1996 were announced by Strathclyde Passenger Transport Authority. This link was intended to be between the airport and St James Station on the existing Glasgow–Gourock line, with a suggested completion date of 2000. The plan, however, was abandoned the following year.

BA suspended their Paris link for the winter of 1994/1995, and shortly after this, in late March, Lufthansa and Air France announced they were pulling out of their weekday serv-

Air Canada A340-313 C-FTNQ which had been diverted in on a medical emergency in August 2005 whilst flying from Heathrow to Calgary. (Fred Seggie)

ices to Glasgow. Air France had previously introduced A320s on their Glasgow–Paris route in spring 1994. Lufthansa withdrew their service to Frankfurt on 24 March 1995 with Boeing 737 D-ABMA operating the final service. However, British Midland Commuter provided week-end connections after that date using Lufthansa flight numbers. This bad news was offset by Sabena announcing that they were doubling their weekday services to Glasgow and Edinburgh from Brussels. This doubling involved dedicating a service to each airport with their BAe 146/RJ85s. Previously the twice-daily service visited both airports and the change reduced travelling time for some passengers by an hour. Sabena had leased BAe1-11s G-AVMI and G-AVMK (in Sabena colours) from British World Airlines during 1995 to operate the service.

A highly significant event took place on 10 November 1995. That morning a Boeing 737-200 took off from Luton Airport for Glasgow to launch Easyjet's first passenger service. At the time many people in the aviation industry would not have thought that twenty-eight-year-old Stelios Haji-Ioannou would stand much chance competing against Ryanair, British Airways, British Midland and Air UK on flights between Scotland and the London area. Also against him was the fact that at the time of the first flight from Luton to Glasgow the airline did not possess its own operating certificate and had to lease aircraft and crew from Air Foyle to start operations. However, after a marketing campaign which invited people to fly to Scotland for the price of a pair of jeans (£29 one way) the inaugural flight was full. From the start of the three-times-a-day Luton–Glasgow service Easyjet went from strength to strength to become one of the leading low-cost operators in Europe.

After Northwest Airlines and United Airlines ceased operating from Glasgow, Airtours moved into the now vacant St Andrews House. By 1995 Airtours were operating five flights a week, up from three weekly flights the previous winter.

On top of the United and Northwest withdrawals, American Airlines announced it would not operate Glasgow–Chicago from the winter 1995/96 schedule.

To counter the withdrawal of these transatlantic services BA started a Glasgow–New York (JFK)–Boston service using dedicated Boeing 757s G-BPEC and G-BPEE with twenty Club World and 141 economy seats from January 1995.

Also on the transatlantic routes Air Canada increased their frequencies to daily for Glasgow–Toronto and doubled their frequency to Western Canada with a twice-weekly Glasgow–Calgary–Vancouver service.

British World Airlines BAe 146 G-BTZN operated Air UK's new Stansted service which started on 23 October 1995.

The Aer Lingus Commuter division replaced the fifty-seat Fokker 50 with the larger 110 seat BAe 146-300 on the Dublin route, which was handled by the jet aircraft from June 1995 onwards, although the odd lightly loaded flight was still operated by the Fokker 50. Part of the reason for the increase in capacity was to develop Dublin as an alternative hub to Heathrow for passengers wanting to fly to Boston and New York. USA customs clearance was offered at Dublin to make it an attractive alternative. It was also partly in response to the threat from Ryanair which had started operating low fare flights from Prestwick to Dublin. Manx Airlines had already introduced a daily (except Saturdays) Glasgow–Dublin service the previous year on 29 March 1994, but this was terminated in 1995 due to poor loads, with Loganair stepping in to take over the route.

There were a number of flights associated with the Borussia Dortmund v Rangers match over 26 September to 29 September, plus the arrival on 27 September of an Adjarian Airlines TU134, UR65073, bringing Dinamo Batumi to play Celtic FC. Adjarian were a Georgian Airline which survived only one year of operation.

There were no less than six emergency landings and diversions during 1995 including KLM Boeing 747 PH-BUI in January 1995 which diverted to Glasgow with a disruptive passenger who had to be handcuffed to his seat.

A proposal had been made in 1995 to start operating a Glasgow–Sydney (via Manchester) service by Excalibur Airways on behalf of Globespan. The flights were to have been between November 1996 and March 1997. However, Excalibur went into receivership in June 1996. They also received adverse publicity over safety fears, which did not help matters.

At the end of virtually every year (October to November) Icelandair doubled its services to Glasgow. In 1996 they increased from three to six flights a week. The previous year a survey had shown that it was estimated that 4 per cent of the population of Iceland were reported to have shopped in Glasgow with Lager costing a sixth of the price it was in Iceland. Long time airport employee Tom Boyle reported that whenever there was an Icelandair flight to Glasgow Hills shops in the transit area would sell out their stock of Quality Streets!

A doubling of services on their route to Luton was instigated by Easyjet from 28 October 1996 when they increased their flights from two to four a day. The service had gone from

Adjarian Airlines TU 134-A3 UR65073 brought in Dinamo Batumi for a match against Celtic and was at the airport on 26/27 September 1995. (Gerry McLaughlin)

strength to strength and continued to grow. British Midland was keen to attract the premium business class passengers on their Heathrow shuttle and introduced a dedicated business class service from September 1996.

Loganair had been absorbed into British Regional Airways in October 1996. Manx Airlines (Europe) changed its name to British Regional Airways, initially as a centralising exercise, with some job losses at Glasgow. The managing director of Loganair, Scott Grier, held talks in October about a management buy-out from British Regional which came to fruition when the buy out was completed on 1 March 1997. Loganair continued to operate with five BN Islanders and one Twin Otter under the BA Express banner. Their Short 360s were transferred to British Regional in January 1997.

Heavylift Cargo Airlines started a new Glasgow–Amsterdam freight flight on 4 March 1996 using Lockheed Hercules PK-PLU on an eight-month lease from Pelita Air Service of Indonesia.

An American Airlines Boeing 767, N366AA, was diverted on 11 September 1996 due to a bomb scare en route to Chicago from Heathrow. No bomb was found and the aircraft returned to Heathrow where the passengers spent the night before resuming their journey the following day, only for the aircraft to be diverted again, this time to Goose Bay, because a passenger had a suspected heart attack.

Some notable visitors during 1996 included the first visit by an IL76 RA76401 on 12 April operating for Heavylift, a Singapore Airlines Boeing 747-400 9V-SMF arrived on a medical emergency on 26 February (after a member of the cabin crew hit her head working in the galley and suffered concussion), two visits by Czech Air Force TU134 1407 in August, French Air Force A-310 422 and Royal flight BAe 146 ZE700 brought in Jacques Chirac and Prince Charles respectively on 16 May.

During the 1997/98 financial year, work began on phase two of the Cargo Village. This comprised two buildings, the first of 3,900 sq. m (which had already been partly let before completion) and a second building of 19,915 sq. m which were both completed in 1999.

Glasgow Flying Club moved to its new clubhouse and dedicated ramp on the north side with tie downs for six aircraft and a parking area for visitors. Shortly after this Execair moved into the new business centre on the site of the old Flying Club.

BA started a new Glasgow–Gatwick service in April 1997. This was not viewed with great favour by Air UK as they felt there was not enough traffic to sustain both their service and the six times daily new service introduced by BA. Air UK withdrew from the route at the end of March 1997. At the other end of the scale, Bright Air (Holland) commenced a six times weekly Edinburgh–Glasgow–Carrickfinn service from late December 1997 using Cessna 406s.

From 30 March 1997, offering a return fare of £59, Jersey European Airways launched a twice-daily Birmingham–Glasgow service in competition with British Airways. Jersey European also introduced a Glasgow–Birmingham–Jersey–Guernsey service from 27 October 1997. Another airline offering cheap fares was Euroscot Express who started services to Bournemouth (using BAe 1-11 G-AVMT) from both Glasgow and Edinburgh offering a one way fare of £39. Easyjet again increased the number of daily flights to Luton from four to five each weekday from 14 February 1997. As part of a promotion, Easyjet handed out bottles of Whisky to all full fare paying passengers on Scottish routes in February 1997. This highlighted the extent of the 'encouragement' given by Easyjet and its competitors to company employee passengers to select the more expensive options when they were travelling on business.

A service which had been operated several years before by SAS was resurrected when Norwegian operator Wideroe started a five-days-a-week service from Glasgow to Stavanger using DH8s from 27 October 1997, with LN-WFC operating the first three flights. Another new service was Glasgow–Innsbruck operated by Tyrolean Airways Fokker F70s from December 1997.

There was a spate of 'smaller' routes being opened in 1998 including a new service to the Faroes from June to August by Atlantic Airways. Debonair commenced ski charters to

CAA Flight Calibration Service Hs 748 Srs 2/238 G-AVXJ taxiing to the runway for ILS checking, 12 November 1997. (Fred Seggie)

Boeing 767-223ER N334AA American Airlines arriving from Chicago on 28 October 1998. American Airlines operated the Glasgow–Chicago service from 1990 until 2006, with breaks. N334AA achieved world-wide notoriety by being the aircraft flown into the North Tower of the World Trade Centre on '9/11'. (Gerry McLaughlin)

Chambery during the winter (from Christmas 1998) on Saturdays using BAe 146s, KLM UK (formed in 1997 with Air UK) introduced a Glasgow–London City Airport service on 25 October 1998. Other changes included Loganair taking over Glasgow–Inverness–Kirkwall–Lerwick from British Regional from 26 October 1998.

In February 1998 RAM (Royal Air Maroc) operated a series of flights taking car dealers to Morocco for the launch of the 1998 Vauxhall/Opel Astra. The aircraft involved in this were Boeing 757 CN-RMT, Boeing 737 CN-RMG, Boeing 737 CN-RNB and Boeing 747 CN-RGA. Jersey European services to Glasgow became all-jet from 18 May 1998. The airline also applied to serve Jersey in the spring of 1999. Monarch Airlines operated Glasgow–Porlamar in Venezuela using their DC10-30 G-DMCA in June and July 1998.

New international services in 1998/99 included Continental Airlines to New York (Newark) with Boeing 757 N14115 operating the first service on 16 July 1998, and Paphos by Air 2000. British Airways confirmed the return of summer only flights to New York's JFK airport five times a week from 1 June 1998, but the extension to Boston was dropped. On the Canadian side, Canada 3000 introduced the first A330-200s in Europe during the summer of 1998 with two flights on Fridays. The first routed Toronto–Glasgow–Calgary-Vancouver arrived in the morning and the second Vancouver–Calgary–Glasgow–Toronto in the late afternoon.

One old-timer visiting on 8 May 1998 was N500EJ, a DC4 belonging to the Berlin Aircraft Historical Foundation. This was followed later in the year by N494TW, a Lockheed Constellation belong to the 'Save a Connie' organisation which arrived on 18 June.

Work was carried out during the winter to resurface and strengthen the main 05/23 runway and also to replace and realign the ground lighting system. Preparation work commenced on 18 October 1999 with the main work starting on 1 November, and was completed by the end of March the following year. The main runway was closed from 1 November to 23 December and 6 January to 31 March between the hours 22.30 and 05.40. There were also restrictions to airfield length and lighting. BN Islander flights used a 500m strip on taxiway Alpha demonstrating its STOL (Short Take Off and Landing) capabilities.

Continental Airlines upgraded their Boeing 757s to DC10s during the summer 1999 schedule. A Continental Airlines DC10, N87070, had already arrived on 25 February 1999 from Gatwick to pick up Glasgow passengers bound for Newark on a Continental Boeing 757 which had been damaged by ground equipment.

A new service started on 28 March 1999 to London City Airport by Suckling Airways, replacing KLM UK. The first flight was undertaken by Dornier 328 G-BWWT. This was also the first visit to Glasgow by Suckling Airways, which was re-launched as ScotAirways following investment by transport operator Stagecoach.

Euroscot Express joined the long list of airlines which had gone into receivership when they ceased operations in June 1999. They had been using Gill Airways to operate their services and Gill completely took over the Euroscot Express routes almost immediately. Before their demise Euroscot had hoped to use a Fokker 100 on their routes, but it was not to be.

Some interesting visitors in 1999 included a US Marshals service Boeing 727, N7128T, operating for the US Department of Justice, which arrived from Halifax on its way to Turin, Concorde G-BOAE which made an overshoot on 1 July in company with the Red Arrows, three Aeroflot IL76s in November with RA76478 making two visits, and finally, the venerable DC3 G-AMRA which made what was expected to be her final flight before being withdrawn from use when she arrived from Stansted on her way to Coventry. However, Air Atlantique kept the aircraft flying for a few more years after this and in 2003 was operating for Highland Airways on their mail run to Benbecula and Stornoway.

Into the Twenty-first Century

The first movement of the new millennium was, appropriately enough, Loganair BN Islander G-BLNW, which landed at 00.16. The airport started the twenty-first century with passenger numbers approaching a healthy 7 million per annum. There was, however, moderate activity on the growth of services. Eastern Airways started a Norwich to Glasgow via Humberside service on 6 February 2000 using Jetstream 31s, but this was dropped as it was not a success. Channel Express started a new Glasgow–Stansted–Paris (Charles De Gaulle) service to act as a feeder for Federal Express services at Paris after they (Federal Express) announced their withdrawal from Prestwick in 2000. Also starting a new service in October 2000 to Paris (Charles De Gaulle) via Birmingham was Jersey European, code sharing with Air France, using Canadair CRJ200s.

In July 2000 BA Concorde G-BOAF passed through on its way from New York JFK to Heathrow whilst four days later a corporate Boeing 737 N147AW brought the singer Tina

Spanair MD83 EC-GXU with starboard undercarriage stuck in the grass. Procedures for backtracking were changed after this incident on 19 January 2001. (Fred Seggie)

Virgin Atlantic B747-41R G-VAST departing to Gatwick empty after an inbound flight from Orlando on 29 July 2007. (Fred Seggie)

Turner to Glasgow. Two other visitors which were being ferried from India to the USA earlier in the year were Beech 99Ds which had been bought from an Indian operator and given new US registrations N3221A and N3119U but still retained their old livery of Gujarat Airways.

Glasgow was not unaffected by the events of 11 September 2001. After the closure of US airspace that day, four aircraft en route to the USA were diverted to the airport, including KLM Boeing 747 PH-BFG. Despite the events of 9/11, which had a severe effect on passenger numbers in the latter half of 2001, record traffic growth continued in 2001/2002 and the 7 million passenger mark was passed for the first time. Most of this passenger growth was

SX-BVN B757 Air Scotland on 23 March 2003. By a historical quirk in 1948, Scottish Airlines operated Consolidated Liberator transports (registered SX-DAA and DAB) flying for a Greek company, Hellenic Airlines! (Fred Seggie)

BA A320-111 G-BUSD lifts off on 12 April 2005 on the Heathrow shuttle service. The buildings in the background are the long-established Babcocks Engineering Plant at Renfrew – now Mitsubishi-Babcock Ltd. (Allen McLaughlin)

due to the strong low-cost airline sector. To help meet this demand, a £13 million 2000 space multi-storey car park with direct access to the terminal was constructed and completed in May 2002. £1.5 million was spent on a new hangar to provide additional aircraft maintenance and engineering facilities.

One victim of the 9/11 attacks was Canada 3000 which had taken over Royal Airlines Canada in 2001. They operated services to Toronto, Halifax and Vancouver. The daily Toronto service had already been severely cut back in July 2001 after low bookings, and they went under in November. Although not the best known of airlines, Canada 3000 at the time of their operation was the world's largest charter airline serving ninety-one destinations worldwide with a fleet of sixty-eight aircraft.

Air Canada withdrew its Toronto service for the winter of 2001/2002 which was the first time in forty years it had broken its service. Aer Lingus also reduced their service to Dublin from four daily flights to three. Aer Lingus was struggling to survive at the time and this was part of the many cutbacks the airline was forced to make in order to remain viable. Gill Airways, which had taken over from the defunct Euroscot Express in 1999, went into receivership themselves on 20 September after the Bank of Scotland withdrew financial support at short notice.

There was more positive news in other areas. A new airline, Aerotrans, started a weekly service in June 2001 to Larnaca via Newcastle, initially using Air Atlanta Boeing 747s but thereafter using Excel Airways Boeing 767s. Easyjet started two new services to Belfast and Amsterdam on 21 August 2001. Both enjoyed initial success and the Belfast service was increased to four daily from 3 September and the Amsterdam service to twice daily.

Go were another airline which increased services from Glasgow during 2001. Go Fly (trading as Go) and had been formed by BA three years previously to compete with low-cost carriers like Ryanair, Easyjet and Debonair. They increased their Gatwick–Stansted service to five flights daily from 25 March 2001 and also started a new service to Belfast from 4 May 2001 using a leased Titan Airways BAe 146 before replacing it in August 2001 with their own aircraft. Go also started a new Glasgow–Bristol service in the summer which caused Brymon Airways, already operating the route, to increase their schedule to no less than six flights a day to meet the challenge. Go had already been involved in a fare war with Ryanair on the Glasgow–Dublin route which they (Go) pulled out of in March 2002. Go were eventually bought by Easyjet in 2002 for a deal worth £374 million when Easyjet was looking to expand.

BA announced the merger of Brymon and British Regional Airlines to form British Airways Cityexpress. This resulted in one flight a day to Birmingham being dropped from October 2001 and the BRT Jetstream 41 and EM5 used on the Glasgow–Cork service being replaced by a Brymon DH8 also from October 2001. October 2001 also saw Airtours changing their title to MyTravel.

Two unusual Boeing 767 visitors in December 2001 were I-VEIY in Air Europe colours operating a charter to Cancun from Milan and LOT SP-LOB which was diverted in whilst en route to Warsaw from New York on a medical emergency.

Arguably, the main event of the year 2002 for Glasgow, in terms of football and aviation, was the UEFA Champions League Final on 15 May 2002 between Real Madrid and Bayer Leverkusen. It had been twenty-six years since the last event had been held in Glasgow. The aircraft involved were supposed to have been split between the three Lowland airports, with the Germans going to Prestwick and the Spanish to Edinburgh and Glasgow. However, both German and Spanish flights ended up at Prestwick. A total of over 100 flights descended on Glasgow with the first arrival on 15 May at 06.11 being Air Europa Boeing 737 EC-HBN. Commercial aircraft were parked on the north side of the airport and on runway 10/28 along with general aviation traffic on the south side as well as utilising spare apron space around the British Airways hangar. There were delays of up to an hour in disembarking passengers onto buses for transfer across the main runway. Six football charter Boeing 737s arrived between 10.50 and 11.40. The flow of executive aircraft was constant throughout the day, with King Juan Carlos arriving in Spanish Air Force Falcon 900 T18-2 at 17.37. Most of the general aviation flights had departed by 01.00 that night. One of the last aircraft to leave was Iberia Boeing 757 EC-HDR. With the Spanish press on board the aircraft made a low pass over the Hampden area at around 2,000ft before departing for home. Another football match between Celtic and Celta Vigo in December 2002 saw twelve chartered aircraft flying from Glasgow to Vigo or Santiago, which was more representative of the usual number of aircraft involved in football charters.

BAe Systems had operated Glasgow–Southampton–Glasgow–Warton flights on Mondays and Warton–Glasgow–Southampton flights on Fridays, with BAe 146 G-BLRA, which ceased on 28 June 2002, leaving only Be200 G-VSBC operating between Barrow and Glasgow twice on Wednesdays and once on Fridays, which was changed in November to Monday, Wednesday and Friday. G-VSBC had been operating Vickers flights since 1993.

Air Canada returned for the summer season on 10 April 2002 with a three-days-a-week schedule to Toronto. Boeing 767 C-GHLK operated the first service. Continental upgraded to

4X-AOT Boeing 737 IAI Israeli Aircraft Industries Radar Test Bed on 25 July 2005, resembling a flying hedgehog with a mass of aerials and sensors. The company became Israeli Aerospace Industries on 6 November 2006. (Fred Seggie)

Boeing 767s on 16 April 2002 for their Newark service. American Airlines also resumed their daily Chicago summer service using Boeing 767s, with the first flight on 2 May 2002 being undertaken by N386AA. Highland Airways took over the Loganair mail run for Glasgow–Benbecula–Stornoway Glasgow on 19 August 2002. Prime Airlines A300 G-HLAD was present on 8 and 9 September 2002 making one of its last flights as the airline ceased operations a few days later on 13 September 2002. G-HLAD was the only aircraft owned by the airline. Prime Airlines itself was an attempt by Heavylift Cargo Airlines to operate passenger charters. However, Heavylift also ran into financial difficulties before they too ceased trading in September, although the joint venture with Air Foyle continued separately. Another final flight during 2002 was by Cougar Leasing Boeing 727 G-OPMN which operated a number of football charters during October culminating on 14 October in a flight arriving in Glasgow from Iceland – the last passenger revenue flight of a UK registered Boeing 727.

Some interesting visitors in 2002 included Jet trainer L39 Albatros ES-YLN passing through on 28 June on its way from Guernsey to Prestwick making the first ever visit of its type, Air Bosna MD81 T9-AAC on 22 and 25 July, Kirgyz International A300 on 17 July, with the highlight of the year probably being China Airlines Boeing 747-400 B-2472 which arrived from Heathrow on a low-key Government visit before departing to Beijing on 31 May.

The Government White Paper of 16 December 2003 set out the proposed future for air travel in the UK. A new parallel runway was proposed for either Glasgow or Edinburgh initially, but this plan was altered to allow the possibility of both airports getting new runways to cater for the expected growth in air travel. The possibility of a central Scotland airport was examined yet again and dismissed.

Air Scotland was a new start up charter airline with Boeing 757s SX-BVM and SX-BVN. SX-BVN operated its first flight on 29 March 2003. The airline had a number of difficulties during its operation including the impounding of SX-BVN by BAA at Glasgow. Air Holland was then subcontracted to operate their services with Boeing 757 PH-AHE, followed by more leasing of aircraft.

There were a large number of football charters in 2003, with the largest (in numbers) being the UEFA Cup Final in Seville with Celtic playing Porto on 21 May. One interesting football charter was Antonov AN74 YL-RAF for the Kaunas FC/Celtic match over 5–7 August.

Basler BT-67 Turbo-67 C-GAWI of the Alfred Wegener Institute diverted in for fuel on 15 July 2008. The institute carries out scientific research in the Arctic and Antarctic. (Fred Seggie)

Another unusual football visitor was KMV TU154 RA-85722 which arrived on 9 October in connection with a Scotland/Lithuania match. There were seventy-three chartered aircraft involved in the UEFA Cup Final including Air Atlanta, Corsair and European Air Charter Boeing 747s, Azzura Air and Thomas Cook Belgium A320s, My Travel Denmark A330s and Neos Italy Boeing 737 being used to transport about 20,000 fans to and from the match. After the match it is estimated that 16,000 fans arrived back on 21 May, making it the busiest day in the airport's history. The figure excluded supporters who travelled from other UK airports to Seville and also those who used low-cost carriers and regular flights (AMM, Britannia Airways, My Travel) to Malaga and Faro.

Scottish niche market operator Flyglobespan moved their operations from Prestwick to Glasgow on 1 November 2003.

Another sporting event beginning on 7 July was the Scottish Open at Loch Lomond which saw the arrival of a number of executive jets including Gulfstream 4SP N526EE belonging to Ernie Els' and Phil Mickelson's Gulfstream 2TT N800PM.

BA Boeing 777 G-VIIM covered two Glasgow–Gatwick services after an aircraft became unserviceable on 4 April 2003. Two Venezuelan Navy CASA 212s, ARBV-0204 and ARBV-0206, passed through over 15–16 May. They had originally travelled through Glasgow on delivery as TR-0204 and TR-0206 in April and June 1981 respectively and had been sent back to Spain for rework. There was an overshoot by Nimrod MR2 XV254 on 7 June. A naval exercise held in September 2003 brought in a number of naval military aircraft and helicopters over 12–14 September from Denmark, France, the Netherlands, Spain and the Royal Navy. Amongst these were Spanish Navy Cessna 550 U20-3 and US Navy Orion 149676. Two other visitors of note were Netjets BBJ N191QS which brought singer Mariah Carey to Glasgow over 23–26 October and BA Boeing 777 G-YMMM which arrived with Prime Minister Tony Blair on 8 December 2003. G-YMMM later crashed while landing at Heathrow on 17 January 2008. The two events are believed to be unrelated!

The centenary of powered flight on 17 December 2003 was celebrated by UGSAS with a fly-by of their four Grob Tutors and a visit by Chipmunk G-AORW.

In June 2004 Glasgow's low-cost airline check-in facility, known as T2, was officially opened by Alistair Darling MP. Designed to handle over 1.5 million passengers per annum, it was built

Glasgow Flying Club Piper PA-38-112 Tomahawk G-BNIM on 21 May 2009. Formed at Renfrew in 1963 and located on the north side of the airport, the club is one of the oldest in the UK, and continues to thrive.

to attract and accommodate the growth of low-cost airlines. Extra capacity was also added to the main terminal.

Glasgow achieved a major milestone in July 2004 by becoming the first Scottish airport to handle over 1 million passengers in a month (1,007,400 passengers) with 16 July being the busiest day. The figures for the month were assisted in no small part by thousands of golf fans passing through the airport for the British Open at Troon. Overall for the year, passengers handled were up by 5.7 per cent to 8.6 million. The BAA route development fund assisted in the formation of new European and North American routes, including those to Philadelphia, Ottawa, Barcelona, Prague and Geneva.

2004 was a year which could be summed up as one of strong growth for the airport On 10 April 2004 Emirates launched a new long-haul service to Dubai with A330 A6-EAQ. This was Scotland's first direct link to the Gulf. Emirates subsequently announced a 50 per cent increase in capacity from Glasgow in response to surging demand. From October 2005 Emirates started to operate Boeing 777-300 on the route. Emirates Skycargo also gave Scottish exporters their first direct access to the Gulf. In addition to the new Emirates service US Airways started a new scheduled service to Philadelphia from 11 May, with Boeing 767 N649US operating the first service.

With more international routes than ever before, international traffic rose by almost 13 per cent. Czech Airlines started a new daily scheduled service to Prague on 31 October. There was an unfortunate start to the new Prague service when Boeing 737 OK-XGB was hit by a tug and airbridge on 2 November and Boeing 737 OK-XGW was flown in to replace it. Continental Airlines and Flyglobespan all expanded their services. Flyglobespan in particular based three Boeing 737s at Glasgow for their significant programme starting on 1 April 2004. Malmo Aviation continued their regular summer programme with flights to Malmo and Salzburg, although Rimini was not operated as it had been in the past. Both Zoom Airlines and Thomas Cook Airlines increased their flights to Canada with Thomas Cook basing two Boeing 757s at Glasgow to cover their schedules. Despite First Choice and Thomas Cook Airlines being adversely affected by hurricanes in Florida holiday charters were strong for the year with Excel Airways operating an extra twenty-eight flights over the school holidays in October 2004.

These increases in all areas can be seen in the fact that on Monday 28 June 2004 there were sixteen widebody aircraft movements.

On the domestic side Flybe started a new service to Belfast City Airport on 28 March 2004 with DHC8 G-JEDY undertaking the first flight, and EU Jet started a new scheduled weekday service to and from Manston on 4 October 2004.

On the back of this strong growth more retail outlets opened in the terminal bringing the total to over forty shops and fifteen food outlets. Celtic and Rangers opened their first ever stores side by side in June 2004.

Gama Aviation Beech 200s G-BPPM and G-HAMA continued to operate air ambulance flights with 21 services in January 2004 alone.

The idea of a rail link to the airport was again raised and consultation opened in November 2004.

Interesting visitors for 2004 included Heliair Antonov 12 carrying the instruments of the BBC Symphony Orchestra to and from Tallinn on 15 and 20 March while the musicians travelled on Estonian Airways Boeing 737 ES-ABH. Celtic's match in Barcelona on 25 March saw no less than nine aircraft returning to Glasgow early the following day, all arriving within thirty-five minutes of each other. Probably the first Northwest Airlines A330 to be seen in the UK landed on 15 April when N805NW, travelling from Amsterdam to Detroit, landed with a medical emergency. Later that day Cessna 525 PH-DOL arrived with a replacement medical kit for the A330. BAe 125 HZ-BL2 passed through on 27 April and 6 May, and this was the second executive jet for the Bin Laden Construction Group and was the subject of a press article. A German maritime reconnaissance Breguet Atlantic 61+16 visited on 31 May. A fire on board a Canadian submarine and its recovery to Faslane brought in four RCAF aircraft over 9–15 October: CC144s 144616 and 144615, CC130 130333 and CC150 15003. Greek Falcon 2000 SX-DCF visited on 30–31 October, and finally, Air France cargo Boeing 747 F-BPVZ diverted in on 2 December because of fog at Prestwick. The final movement for 2004 (2316 from Inverness) and the first for 2005 (0018 to Aberdeen) were once again Air Ambulance services.

Sadly, the Air Ambulance Service suffered another tragedy on 15 March 2005. Loganair's BN Islander G-BOMG was operating an Air Ambulance Service to Campbeltown when all contact was lost with the aircraft at 01.15. The wreckage of the aircraft was found in the sea 7.7 miles from Campbeltown. Unfortunately there were no survivors.

In June 2005 work began on an extension to the international pier. This was the first stage of a £50 million redevelopment of the main terminal building. Four new aircraft stands were built bringing the total to thirty-eight, and planning work was begun during the year to increase this figure.

During the year 2005 Euromanx services continued to function through a variety of leased operators and aircraft. Thirty-five different aircraft had in fact been noted since they started services. Air Scotland experienced a cash crisis over 13–19 October and its Boeing 757 was impounded at Edinburgh on 13 October due to an unpaid fuel bill. A new holiday charter service was started by Karthago Airlines with Boeing 737 TS-IEC operating the first flight on 1 June 2005 to Monastir.

Flybe started a daily Glasgow–Liverpool service from 27 March 2005 which was increased to twice daily from 16 June. However, the service did not prove to be as popular as anticipated and the route was dropped by Flybe at the end of the summer 2005 season.

The October 2005 school holidays gave another boost to passenger figures along with football charters at the same time which saw Belavia TU154 EW-85748 at Glasgow from 6 to 8 October. On the scheduled side SN Brussels Airlines started a nine-times-a-week service to Brussels from 2 June 2005 with BAe 146RJ85 OO-DJR undertaking the first service. Continental Airlines added four flights a week to their New York Newark service, making a total of eleven flights a week. A major boost to international services was the start of PIA's (Pakistan International Airlines) new services to Lahore (on Wednesdays) and Islamabad (on Saturdays), both via Dubai. A-310 AP-BDZ operated the first three flights on 16, 19 and 23 November 2005.

VLM (Flightline) Bae 146-300/RJ00 G-BPNT, VLM's first jet. As G-BPNT it has been a regular visitor to airports throughout Europe and has carried passengers as diverse as the Northern Ireland Football team, Robbie Williams and U2. (Kevin Marchbank)

Air Berlin Boeing 737-76Q D-ABBN on 12 July 2006. The ambitious attempt by Air Berlin to create a mini hub at Stansted for onward flights to Germany was thwarted by increases in UK airport tax. (Charlie Stewart)

Easyjet A-319s started to replace their Boeing 737s on the Glasgow–Bristol and Glasgow–Stansted routes. Unfortunately, CSA the Czech Airline ceased its Prague service at the end of July 2005. Air Canada operated its last scheduled flight to Scotland after over sixty years of service when Boeing 767 C-FVNM departed Glasgow on 1 October 2005. Similarly, American Airlines Boeing 767 N385AM operated the last flight of its summer only schedule on 2 October 2005.

Visitors of note in 2005 included two Norwegian Air Force C130 Hercules (952 and 955) on 3 and 15 May respectively, followed by Netherlands Air Force C130 Hercules G-273 on 8 May, Antonov 12 ER-AXY of Astral Aviation on 13 June, Boeing N88ZL of Lowa Ltd on 5 and 6 July, a test-bed Boeing 737 4X-AOT covered in aerials and an odd nose radome visited on 25 July, and a nostalgic and specially painted (with a commemorative logo) Icelandair DC3 TF-NPK on 11 July to celebrate the sixtieth anniversary of Icelandair's predecessor (Flugfelag Islands) first international flight to Scotland on 11 July 1945 when Catalina TF-ISP arrived at Largs Bay.

N526EE GulfstreamV on 12 July 2008, belonging to the golfer Ernie Els, then playing at the Barclays 2008 Scottish Open Tournament at Loch Lomond. (Charlie Stewart)

On 1 April the new Air Ambulance contract became effective forcing the Loganair BN Islander G-BPCA to stand down and GAMA Aviation took over the Glasgow based duties with Be200 Super King Air G-SASC. G-SASD, the sister aircraft of G-SASC, which visited between 20 and 23 March 2006 to enable paramedics to familiarise themselves with the new aircraft and its kit.

Scottish airline Flyglobespan decided to suspend its domestic UK routes and concentrate on serving international destinations from its main hubs, including Glasgow. They had based five Boeing 737s at Glasgow over most of winter 2005/2006. The Glasgow–London Stansted route, launched in 2005, was stopped at the end of February 2006. New services were started in May of that year from Glasgow to Pula, Mahon, Athens and Heraklion. Flyglobespan's first long-haul route was launched the following month from Glasgow to Orlando. A number of Flyglobespan European services out of Glasgow were combined with Edinburgh for the winter schedule in 2006/2007.

Despite only having started their service a year earlier SN Brussels stopped their lunchtime Brussels flight on 6 January ahead of ceasing the whole service at the end of March 2006. American Airlines also operated their last Chicago service on 30 September 2006 with Boeing 767 N379AA. KLM reduced their Amsterdam service to five flights a week from 28 August 2006 with two Fokker 70s, two Boeing 737s and one Fokker 100, which stopped for the night, operating the five services. The night-stopping Fokker 100 was replaced by a Boeing 737 at the start of the winter 2006/2007 schedule.

Other services continued to do well, however, in particular the new Emirates service to Dubai which now had Boeing 777-200s operating the service six times a week from the end of January 2006. Aer Lingus added five extra flights a week to their Dublin service at the start of their winter 2006/2007 schedule. Air Berlin operated a mix of Fokker 100s and Boeing 737-700s in their ambitious attempt to create a mini hub at Stansted for onward services to Germany. The twice-daily Glasgow–Stansted service started on 16 December 2005, but was dropped before the end of 2007 due to an increase in airport tax which made onward German connections unprofitable.

Heavy snow on 12 March 2006 closed the airport until 16.00 that day causing a number of cancellations, diversions and delays. Even when the airport re-opened, aircraft were still being forced to divert because of a lack of stands.

TF-JMA DHC 8-106 of Flugfelag Islands bringing in a cargo of fish on 26 March 2009. (Fred Seggie)

There were a number of interesting military visitors in 2006: A-310s belonging to the Belgian and French air forces (serials CA-02 and FRADC/418) visited on 12 and 14 January respectively, with Netherlands Air Force DC10 T-235 making no less than four separate visits in February and two more in June along with T-264. Hellenic Air Force C130 Hercules 744 came in on 21 February with a Rolls-Royce engine for overhaul, three RAF Jaguars were present over 2–3 March – XX738, XZ392 and XX835 (a Jaguar T4). A USAF MC130 Hercules 40561 diverted in over 11–13 April because of a hydraulic leak. Swiss Air Force Ce560 T-784 arrived from and departed to Berne on 25–26 July. Non military visitors included HELLO MD90 HB-JIE on 25 June operating an Air Berlin service, Olympic Airways Boeing 737 SX-BKE on 5 July, Boeing 727 N73751 passed through on 5 August for delivery to SAFAIR in South Africa, Titan Airways Boeing 757 G-ZAPX arrived on 24 July with the Rolling Stones for three days. Some well heeled fans of the Rolling Stones arrived on Canadair CL600S N247CK on 25 August, departing the following day. Corsair Boeing 747 F-HSEX operated a Thomsonfly service combined with Edinburgh on 27 September to Alicante. Israeli airline Sun D'or International Boeing 757 4X-EBY operated a football charter over 31 October-3 November. There was an Icelandic invasion on 5 November when no less than seven Icelandair Boeing 757s were diverted because of bad weather at Keflavik. Bad weather also finished the year 2006 in Glasgow when storm force winds on Hogmanay caused diversions to Newcastle and Manchester.

2007 started with strong southwesterly winds for a number of days causing the diversion of four Boeing 747F freighters from Prestwick along with American Airlines Boeing 777 N750AN which was forced to divert into Glasgow for fuel on 18 January. There were further diversions in February from Prestwick caused by crosswinds which included Atlas Air Boeing 747 N809MC on 28 February.

Flybe took control of BA Connect on 25 March 2007 and leased additional capacity in the form of European Aircharter's Boeing 737s G-CEAE and G-CEAH which were at Glasgow on 26/27 March and 29 March respectively. KLM reverted back to five daily flights from 25 March 2007. Pakistan International had well publicised maintenance issues in the early part of 2007 which led to the first service in March being cancelled and Boeing 777s taking over schedules to Lahore and Islamabad for the rest of the month.

BA Boeing 747-400 G-BNLE on 2 February 2009. The appearance of a BA 747 at Glasgow is usually
a diversion. G-BNLE, which originated in Houston, was diverted in due to heavy snow at Heathrow.
(Allen McLaughlin)

However, the services were both completely suspended in early April, and restarted on
18 April with A-310s TC-SGB and TC-SGC leased from Saga Airlines, though they had been
recently operated by Mahan Air, whose colour scheme the aircraft still partly wore.

SAS made a return to Glasgow with a twice weekly (Mondays and Fridays) Stockholm–
Glasgow service with Boeing 737 LN-RPP operating the first flight on 13 April 2007.

Virgin Atlantic started a short season of flights to Orlando operating Boeing 747s with G-
VAST operating the first flight on 23 June 2007.

Highland Airways started a new charter service on 26 November 2007 with leased Be1900D
OO-PHB on Mondays, Wednesdays, Thursdays and Fridays operating between Glasgow–
Edinburgh–Filton and the return. Be1900D was replaced and the service operated with
Jetstream 31s (G-EIGG and G-JURA) from 5 December 2007.

There was a noticeable reduction in non-based aircraft charter flights which contributed to
an 8 per cent drop in international short-haul passengers as compared to August 2006.

The main runway 05/23 was closed for maintenance from 25–30 March from 23.00 to 05.00
each night.

Interesting visitors in 2007 included Georgian Airlines Boeing 737 4L-TGA on a football
charter on 25 March, Olympic Airways Boeing 717 SX-BOB passed through on 26 April on
its way from Keflavik to Athens in full Spanair colours, appropriately registered Boeing 737
HS-HRH of the Royal Thai Flight visited on 10 July, Chelsea Football Club's owner Roman
Abramovich's Boeing 767 P4-MES was present on 27–28 July, and Montenegro Airlines
Fokker 100s YU-AOT and YU-AOK brought in football supporters from Podgorica – these
were the only two air transport flights between the UK and Montenegro in July 2007 accord-
ing to CAA statistics. Two more interesting football charters from the Balkans followed in
August with JAT Boeing 737s YU-ANV and YU-ANW arriving from Belgrade on 13 and
14 August, a Lufthansa Boeing 747 D-ABTD was diverted in for a medical emergency on
5 August, Lithuanian Airlines Boeing 737 LY-AYQ featured on the list of football charters on
6 and 8 September, Loch Lomond Seaplane Ce208 G-MJDE was noted a number of times

during September on fuel stops, and Boeing 717 HS-PGP of Bangkok Airways passed through on 9–11 December.

The First Minister for Scotland, Alex Salmond, opened a new state of the art security search area on 3 December 2008. This was part of an eighteen-month £31 million terminal extension adding an extra 4,000m3 to the Skyhub.

Two major airlines collapsed in 2008: Zoom, which served five Canadian destinations from Glasgow, and XL Airways, which served over a dozen holiday resorts in the Mediterranean and Orlando from Glasgow. Air Malta dropped its scheduled service to Malta in December 2008 and Flybe dropped its Newquay service in 2008, although Air South West continued to operate on the route. There was more bad news for Glasgow at the end of 2008 with the proposal by British Airways to axe 135 Glasgow-based cabin crew jobs, with the staff being offered either a transfer to Heathrow or voluntary redundancy.

The bad news was offset by the start of new services including Easyjet to Faro, the resumption of PIA's twice weekly service to Faisalabad and Lahore on 2 April 2008, with A-310s and Air Transat adding four additional A-310 weekly flights to Toronto, in addition to the six Thomas Cook services flown by Boeing 757s. Bmi Baby also started a three-times-a-week service to Knock from 13 February. Continental Airlines celebrated ten years of services at Glasgow on 16 July 2008. Interesting visitors through the year included VT-IAH and VT-VJM A-319s on 7 April and 14 April, HS-TGO Boeing 717 of Bangkok Air, RAF Hawks XX195 XX245 XX325 for a flypast at Hampden on 24 May, and United Airways Boeing 747-400 N118UA for a medical diversion on 4 July. Finally, one aircraft involved in two diversions into Glasgow within six weeks was Delta Boeing 757 N706TW. On 24 October she diverted in from Frankfurt to New York (spending time in the British Airways hangar) and was then diverted in again from Brussels to New York on 3 December.

Terrorism

After the events of 9/11 most of the anti-terrorist measures put in place were generally aimed at the airside of airport operations. However, that was to change on 30 June 2007 when a Jeep

Flyglobespan Boeing 737-300 G-GSPN on 12 April 2005. Scottish-based Flyglobespan continue to go from strength to strength and now have a comprehensive coverage of the main charter destinations for both winter and summer schedules. (Allen McLaughlin)

Cherokee, loaded with gas cylinders was driven into the front of the Glasgow terminal building by two Islamic terrorists, Kafeel Ahmed and Bilal Abdulla.

The attack took place on one of the busiest weekends of the year. The airport was closed from 15.20 on 30 June and reopened the following morning. It took a further couple of days to clear the backlog. There was substantial fire damage to the front of the terminal building although, thankfully, nobody was killed in the attack. Kafeel Ahmed died of burn injuries one month later and Bilal Abdulla was sentenced to life imprisonment in December 2008.

Another area related to terrorism and aviation was the subject of Rendition flights. Rendition or Extraordinary Rendition flights were defined as the practice of national governments moving prisoners internationally. From 2002 Glasgow saw a significant number of aircraft passing through which were alleged to have been involved in these controversial flights.

The Future

There are plans to close the smaller 10/28 runway and change its status for use as a taxiway. The runway only handled 257 movements in 2007. It is also proposed to develop the area to the north of this runway on the western side of the main runway.

In May 2008 Ferrovial (BAA's majority Spanish owners, holding 62 per cent of BAA) ran into financial difficulties and considered selling not only Gatwick, which had been a possibility for some time, but also Glasgow. In the event, in December 2008 the Office of Fair Trading suggested that one of the Scottish airports owned by BAA, Edinburgh, should be sold.

In the immediate future, work is expected to start in 2010 on a £130 million viaduct over the M8 at Paisley for the new rail link. The costs of the proposed rail link soared to £454 million (including £60 million for separate signal work) from £247 million, and the expected completion date was put back by two years to 2013, the year before the Commonwealth Games come to Glasgow.

On the airside Flyglobespan are launching a new weekly Glasgow–Halifax summer service in 2009. Emirates Airways are expected to increase their service to twice-daily with the second service expected to route Dubai–Glasgow–New York in 2009.

On the holiday front the loss of Zoom and XL from the schedules in 2008 will be partly made up by the offering of 25,000 seats by Sunways Holidays of Manchester in partnership with BMI flying to Spain and Portugal.

For many years Abbotsinch was considered as Scotland's premier airport in terms of passengers and fixed wing movements. For the first time ever Edinburgh has overtaken Glasgow to hold the number one spot. Surveys in 2008 showed that 22 per cent of Edinburgh passengers originated in the Glasgow catchment area, although 16 per cent of Glasgow passengers originated in the Edinburgh catchment area. Over the past five years or so both passenger and air transport numbers had been showing declines in some areas and poor growth compared to continual growth at Edinburgh and other regional airports in the UK. Despite this the future still holds promise for Glasgow. The masterplan for the airport produced in October 2006 still expects passenger figures to reach 13.2 million by 2015 and 20.2 million by 2030. Air transport movements are expected grow to 173,300 per annum by 2030. The BAA have earmarked £290 million for a capital investment programme (which includes a new international pier) over ten years from the end of 2006. Much of the future growth is expected to come from international passengers.

APPENDIX I

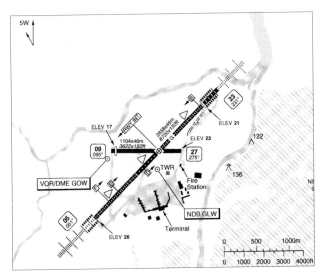

Left: Current layout of Abbotsinch – *not for operational use.* (Courtesy of Euronautical)

Below: Layout of Renfrew after the two runways were built. (Crown Copyright)

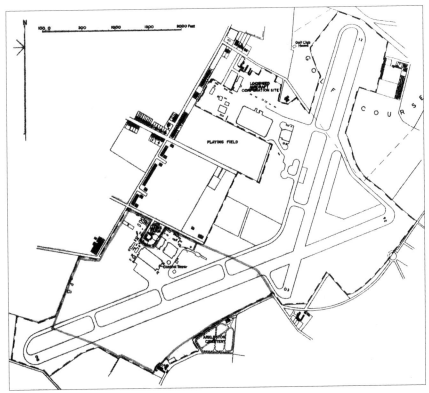

APPENDIX II

Airlines scheduled to depart from Glasgow on 28 February 2009, with destinations shown below:

Aer Lingus
  Dublin

Air Malta
  Malta

Air Southwest
  Newquay
  Plymouth

Air Transat
  Toronto

British Airways
  Barra
  Campbeltown
  London City
  London Gatwick
  London Heathrow
  Londonderry
  Tiree

Bmi
  Birmingham
  Copenhagen
  Leeds/Bradford
  London Heathrow
  Manchester

Bmi baby
  Cardiff
  East Midlands
  Knock

Canterbury Travel
  Kittila

Continental Airlines
  New York (Newark)

Easyjet
  Alicante
  Belfast International
  Berlin Schoenefeld
  Bristol
  Faro
  London Gatwick
  London Luton
  London Stansted
  Malaga
  Palma
  Paris (CDG)

Emirates
  Dubai

Flybe
  Belfast City
  Birmingham
  Cardiff
  Exeter
  Jersey
  La Rochelle
  Manchester
  Newquay
  Southampton

Flyglobespan
   Alicante
   Arrecife
   Barcelona
   Calgary (summer only)
   Dalaman
   Faro
   Hurghada
   Ibiza (summer only)
   Las Palmas
   Malaga
   Orlando (Sanford)
   Palma
   Paphos
   Tenerife (South)
   Toronto (Hamilton)
   Vancouver (summer only)

Goldtrail
   Izmir

Icelandair
   Reykjavik

KLM Cityhopper
   Amsterdam

Loganair
   Benbecula
   Islay
   Isle of Man
   Kirkwall
   Stornoway
   Sumburgh

PIA Pakistan International Airlines
   Faisalabad
   Lahore

Thomas Cook
   Banjul

Thomson Airways
   Funchal
   Palma
   Rovaniemi

US Airways
   Philadelphia (summer only)

Virgin Atlantic Airways
   Orlando (summer only)

Charter Airlines using Glasgow Airport as of 28 February 2009, including destinations:

Summer:

Alicante	Flyglobespan / Thomas Cook Airlines / Thomsonfly
Antalya	Thomas Cook Airlines
Arrecife	Thomas Cook Airlines / Thomsonfly /
Barcelona	Flyglobespan / bmi
Bodrum	Thomas Cook Airlines / Thomsonfly / Onur Air
Bourgas	Thomas Cook Airlines / Thomsonfly /Air–Balkan Holidays
Calgary	Flyglobespan / Thomas Cook Airlines / Air Transat
Cancun	Thomas Cook Airlines / Thomsonfly
Corfu	Thomas Cook Airlines / Thomsonfly
Dalaman	Flyglobespan / Thomas Cook Airlines / Thomsonfly / bmi/ Onur Air / Pegasus Airlines
Faro	Flyglobespan / Thomas Cook Airlines / Thomsonfly
Fuerteventura	Thomas Cook Airlines
Funchal	Thomas Cook Airlines
Halifax	Flyglobespan
Heraklion	Thomas Cook Airlines / Thomsonfly/ bmi/ Euro Cypria Airlines
Hurghada	Flyglobespan

Ibiza	Flyglobespan / Thomas Cook Airlines/ Thomsonfly
Jersey	Flybe
Kos	Thomas Cook Airlines
Larnaca	Thomas Cook Airlines / Thomsonfly / Euro Cypria Airlines
Las Palmas	Flyglobespan / Thomas Cook Airlines / bmi
Las Vegas	Thomas Cook Airlines
Mahon	Thomas Cook Airlines / Thomsonfly
Malaga	Flyglobespan / Thomas Cook Airlines / Thomsonfly
Malta	Thomas Cook Airlines
Monastir	Thomas Cook Airlines
Naples	Thomsonfly
Orlando (Sanford)	Flyglobespan / Thomas Cook Airlines / Thomsonfly
Palma	Flyglobespan / Thomas Cook Airlines / Thomsonfly
Paphos	Flyglobespan / Thomas Cook Airlines / Thomsonfly / bmi
Puerta Plata	Thomas Cook Airlines / Thomsonfly
Punta Cana	Thomsonfly
Reus	Thomas Cook Airlines / Thomsonfly
Rhodes	Thomas Cook Airlines / Thomsonfly
Salzburg	bmi
Sharm El Sheikh	Thomas Cook Airlines / Thomsonfly
Tenerife	Flyglobespan / Thomas Cook Airlines / Thomsonfly / bmi
Toronto	Flyglobespan / Thomas Cook Airlines / Air Transat
Vancouver	Thomas Cook Airlines
Varna	Air-Balkan Holidays
Verona	Thomsonfly
Zakynthos	Thomas Cook Airlines / Thomsonfly

Winter:

Alicante	Flyglobespan/ Thomson / Thomas Cook
Antalya	Thomas Cook
Arrecife	Flyglobespan/ Thomson / Thomas Cook / First Choice
Banjul	Thomas Cook
Barcelona	Flyglobespan
Calgary	British Airways
Dalaman	Flyglobespan
Enontekio, Lappland	European Air Charter★
Faro	Flyglobespan / Thomas Cook / First Choice
Fuerteventura	Thomson / Thomas Cook / First Choice
Funchal	Thomson / First Choice
Geneva	Thomson
Hurghada	Flyglobespan
La Romana	Thomson
Las Palmas	Flyglobespan/ Thomson / Thomas Cook / Air Europa
Lyon	Thomson
Malaga	Flyglobespan
Monastir	Thomson / Thomas Cook / First Choice
Orlando Sanford	Flyglobespan
Palma	Flyglobespan / Thomson / Thomas Cook / First Choice
Paphos	Flyglobespan/ Thomson
Salzburg	Thomson

Sharm El Sheikh	Thomson / Thomas Cook
Tenerife	Flyglobespan/ Thomson / Thomas Cook / Air Europa / First Choice
Toronto	Air Transat
Vancouver	Thomas Cook

*European Air Charter went into liquidation on 30/11/08

APPENDIX III

Passenger Figures and Air Transport Movements 1950–2008:

RENFREW

Year	Passengers '000s	ATMs
1950	138,146	12,788
1951	139,599	10,846
1952	156,916	10,771
1953	210,023	11,910
1954	258,481	13,347
1955	305,574	14,616
1956	373,948	16,211
1957	436,561	19,651
1958	443,481	19,563
1959	528,682	20,161
1960	652,180	22,244
1961	741,394	23,968
1962	854,988	21,940
1963	996,264	22,076
1964	1,150,506	25,355
1965	1,240,066	26,636
1966	1,406,879★	30,907★

ABBOTSINCH

Year	Passengers '000s	ATMs
1967	1,528,980	34,414
1968	1,387,210	31,800
1969	1,610,774	33,889
1970	1,702,555	34,820
1971	1,744,128	36,200
1972	1,880,265	37,823
1973	2,142,437	43,268
1974	1,935,446	42,722
1975★★	1,764,284	35,087
1976	1,976,168	37,370
1977	1,752,470	35,787

1978	2,153,899	4,659
1979	2,360,132	49,150
1980	2,340,398	50,978
1981	2,267,648	49,281
1982	2,407,293	52,848
1983	2,442,458	54,509
1984	2,747,289	55,783
1985	2,696,754	51,385
1986	3,102,844	56,504
1987	3,366,376	58,260
1988	3,635,646	60,484
1989	3,862,000	66,877
1990	4,287,000	70,952
1991	4,154,000	71,985
1992	4,670,000	76,496
1993	5,015,000	77,386
1994	5,456,000	75,633
1995	5,423,000	74,866
1996	5,472,000	75,647
1997	6,012,000	80,066
1998	6,481,000	83,492
1999	6,759,000	86,298
2000	6,923,000	88,732
2001	7,249,000	92,486
2002	7,772,000	88,396
2003	8,118,000	88,732
2004	8,564,000	92,836
2005	8,782,000	97,029
2006	8,830,000	96,753
2007	8,732,000	93,625

★Combined with Abbotsinch
★★BAA from April 1975

APPENDIX IV

Aircraft and squadrons based at RAF Abbotsinch and RNAS Sanderling:

Squadron	From	To	Arrived–Departed	Aircraft
602	Renfrew	Grangemouth	20/01/33–7/10/39	Wapiti, Hart, Hind, Hector, Gauntlet, Spitfire I, Tutor Battle
21	Bircham	Newton Lympne	22/07/36–03/11/36	Hind
34	Bircham	Newton Lympne	30/07/36–03/11/36	Hind
269	Bircham	Newton Eastleigh	30/12/36–17/01/38	Avro MkI Anson
269	Eastleigh	Thornaby	24/03/38–29/09/38	Avro MkI Anson
269	Thornaby	Montrose	06/10/38–25/08/39	Avro MkI Anson
51★	Formed	Closed	07/39–03/09/39	Tiger Moth
607	Usworth	Usworth	12/08/39–24/08/39	Gloster Gladiator
2CP	Formed	Disbanded	18/10/39–27/05/40	Tiger Moth
816	HMS Furious	HMS Furious	17/12/39–25/12/39	Swordfish
818	Hatston	Campbeltown	17/12/39–25/12/39	Swordfish
816	HMS Furious	HMS Furious	04/01/40–19/02/40	Swordfish
TTU★★	Gosport	Turnberry	19/03/40–11/11/42	Swordfish, Beaufort, Botha
801	HMS Furious	Detling	25/05/40–30/05/40	Skua
819	HMS Illustrious	HMS Illustrious	23/07/40–11/08/40	Swordfish
1830	Culham	Disbanded	15/06/53–10/03/57	Avenger, Sea Balliol
418	Flight Formed	HMS Argus	18/07/40–21/07/40	Hurricane
309	Formed	Renfrew	08/10/40–6/11/40	Lysander (Polish)
807	Prestwick	HMS Furious	07/02/41–05/03/41	Fulmar
800	Arbroath	HMS Argus	12/05/41–17/05/41	Fulmar
88★★★	Sydenham	Sydenham	5/41–5/41	Blenheim
816	Eastleigh	HMS Furious	14/06/41–21/06/41	Swordfish
232	Selkirk	Ouston	19/07/41–21/07/41	None
1441★★★★	Flt Formed	Dundonald	14/01/42–19/10/42	Lysander, Anson
232	Gatwick	Gatwick	03/05/42–14/05/42	Mustang, Hurricane
254★★★★★	Dyce	Docking	01/5/42–10/10/42	Beaufighter
225	Thruxton	Thruxton	13/05/42–21/05/42	Mustang, Hurricane
824	Macrihanish	St Merryn	27/05/43–15/06/43	Swordfish
892	Macrihanish	HMS Archer	12/06/43–15/06/43	Wildcat
835	HMS Chaser	HMS Chaser	11/12/43–18/12/43	Sea Hurricane
768	Ayr	Ayr	19/01/44–05/07/45	Various (for DLT)

832	Macrihanish	HMS *Engadine*	12/02/44–27/02/44	Avenger
730	Formed	Ayr	17/04/44–20/11/44	Various
852	HMS *Nabob*	Macrihanish	08/07/44–12/07/44	Avenger, Wildcat
835	Yeovilton	HMS *Nairana*	30/09/44–04/10/44	Wildcat
824	Macrihanish	Lee on Solent	07/10/44–11/10/44	Swordfish, Wildcat
1840	HMS *Speaker*	Ayr	23/12/44–31/12/44	Hellcat
821	Macrihanish	HMS *Trumpeter*	23/06/45–03/07/45	Barracuda
802	Ayr	HMS *Queen*	27/07/45–10/08/45	Seafire
802	HMS *Queen*	Ayr	24/08/45–03/09/45	Seafire
1702	Lee on Solent	HMS *Trouncer*	05/08/45–13/09/45	Sea Otter
602	Reformed	Disbanded	10/05/46–10/03/57	Spitfire, Meteor, Vampire,
804	HMS *Theseus*	HMS *Theseus*	13/02/47–19/02/47	Seafire
1830	Reformed	Donibristle	15/08/47–02/12/50	Firefly
1967	Flt Perth	Perth	05/12/52–02/09/54	Auster
1843	Reformed	Disbanded	28/03/53–10/03/57	Firefly, Avenger
1967	Flt Perth	Perth	02/09/54–10/03/57	Auster
602	Renfrew	Disbanded	18/06/54–10/03/57	Spitfire, Meteor, Vampire

Other Units:

1680 (Western Isles) Communications Flight, 24/05/43–06/03/44, DH Dominie Fokker XXII

Maintenance Test Pilots School (MTPS)

No.6 Aircraft Assembly Unit, July 1940–1943

No.3 Aircraft Packing Pool

Merchant Ship Fighter Unit (Detachment), 06 May 1943–9/43 Sea Hurricane

Universities of Glasgow and Strathclyde Air Squadrons 13 July 1942–1950, 1969–Current

No.4 Air Experience Flight Jan 1997–Current

No.1967 Reserve AOP Flight No 666 Squadron, 05/12/52–02/02/54, 01/09/55–10/03/57

663 Volunteer Gliding School 16/11/59–9/63

*51 E and RFTS

**TTU (Torpedo Training Unit)

***Detachment from Sydenham

****1441 Combined Operations Development Unit became 516 Combined Operation Squadron on 27 April 1943. The following squadrons were attached to 1441 at Abbotsinch:

239 Squadron	02/05/42–14/05/42	NA Mustang Mk1
18 Squadron	13/05/42–15/05/42	Bristol Blenheim
225 Squadron	13/05/42–21/05/42	Hawker Hurricane and NA Mustang I
21 Squadron	20/05/42–22/05/42	Bristol Blenheim IV

*****Detachment from Dyce for TTU

APPENDIX V

Aircraft and squadrons based at RAF Renfrew:

Squadron	Formed	Period of occupancy	Aircraft
602	Abbotsinch	15/09/25–20/1/33	DH9A Avro 504K/N, Fairey Fawn, Westland Wapiti
309 (Polish)★	Dunino	11/11/40–15/05/41	Westland Lysander
602	Abbotsinch	06/49–18/06/54	North American Harvard T2B, Supermarine Spitfire F14/FR14E/F21/F22, Meteor T7, Vampire F3, Vampire FB5

★There is occasionally some confusion over where 309 Squadron started. It was formed on 8 October 1940 at RAF Abbotsinch and moved over to RAF Renfrew to become operational on 11 November 1940. This was due to works being carried out at Renfrew.

APPENDIX VI

Visit to RNAS Abbotsinch by Eric Bucklow, 21 August 1954, with annotations (in italics) giving additional information by Douglas Rough:

PF663 Mosquito PR 34 *with 751 Squadron*
  Watton on that date: perhaps visiting AC
WM976 Sea Hawk *FB3★ 24.8.84 for Hal Far (HF)*
WM974 Sea Hawk *FB3★To HF 24.8.54*
WM977 Sea Hawk *FB3★To HF 23.8.54*
WM940 Sea Hawk *FB3 to 811 Squadron 29.4.55*
WM980 Sea Hawk *FB3★Arrived AC 16.8.54*
WM925 Sea Hawk *FB3★ AC to Glory for shipment to Far East 15.9.54*
WM990 Sea Hawk *FB3★*
XB326 Avenger *AS4★,* coded 356 *but should be 365*
PH408 Oxford★ *601/AC of Scottish Air Division. To AHU Stretton 3.11.54*
XB379 Avenger *AS5★*
WA179/E Vampire *FB5 602 Squadron*
WA182/B Vampire *FB5 602 Squadron*
XB387 Avenger *AS5★*
WD907 Firefly *FR5★ 240/AC of* XB331 Avenger *AS4★ Scottish Air Division*
Sea Prince *611-AC NB. Does not tie up with any known AC Sea Prince at that time.*
  More research needed
VZ812/C Vampire *FB5 602 Squadron*
EZ373 Harvard *III 1830 Squadron AC★*
VZ356 Sea Fury *T.20 actually VZ365 at AC by 8.54, code 234 ??*
VZ664 Sea Hornet *PR22★ NB. During a Test Flight at AC 6.9.54 canopy shattered during gentle pull*
  out from 400kt dive from 4000ft Cat L SOC 17.9.54 to GI airframe
EK?34 ★ *Firebrand TF5 + five others. It is EK634 ex-DO and remains noted AC 8.56 + two wrecks*
  + a/c 239. Other F/brands on AC F/dump at this time were +EK632/633/674/675/744/795 and almost
  certainly EK693 SOC AC 3.7.53 i.e. Eight in total + AC with code 239 (possibly Harvard)
WM973 Sea Hawk *FB3★*
WM923 Sea Hawk *FB3 NB. AC to 811 Squadron LM 19.7.55*
WM978 Sea Hawk *FB3 NB. Reportedly did not arrive at AC until 23.11.55*
WM912 Sea Hawk *FB3 NB. Reportedly left AC for 803 Squadron FD on 14.6.55*
WM964 Sea Hawk *FB3 Mid-air collision with Sabre 4 XB700 near VL 17.8.55*
WM965 Sea Hawk *FB3 from AC to 811 Squadron LM 22.3.55*
TW526 Auster *AOP6 666 Squadron possibly AC-based 1907 Flight*
WB-247 Firefly *5★ Cocooned AC 10.6.53*
VZ656 Sea Hornet *PR22★*

VZ658? Sea Hornet *PR22* ★ *NB. Correct AC was VZ658*
TT210 Sea Hornet *F20*★
TT209 Sea Hornet *F20*★
VR858 Sea Hornet *FR20*★
TT203 Sea Hornet *F20*★
VA879 *Mosquito T3*★ *Stored cocooned at AC. SOC 11.8.55 used for f/fighting practice at AC until 1957*
VA880 *Mosquito T3*★ *Stored cocooned at AC. SOC 11.8.55 used for f/fighting practice at AC until 1957*
VT607 Mosquito *T3*★ *SOC at AC 11.8.55. Remains on AC Fire Dump 1957*
TV954 Mosquito *T3*★ *SOC at AC 11.8.55. Used for f/fighting practice at AC until 1957*
TV964 Mosquito *T3*★ *SOC at AC 11.8.55. Used for f/fighting practice at AC until 1957*
VZ661 Sea Hornet *PR22*★
VZ709 Sea Hornet *FR20*★
WD809 or 889 Firefly *FR5*★ *should be WD889: was ScAir Div c.6.54*
MB505 Firefly *FR1*★*ex-SOC Arbroath 7.6.55: remains at AC by 7.56*
WM906 Sea Hawk *FB3*★ *AC to Ford 30.11.54*

Note: Eric Bucklow retired from BAe Warton where he was a Tornado Test Pilot
This listing is as per his jottings for the day and not grouped by types DAR
AC–Abbotsinch
SOC–Struck off Charge
★–known from official records to have been at AC on 21/8

APPENDIX VII

Part of the function of both Abbotsinch and Renfrew was to act as receiving centres for the considerable number of aircraft arriving and departing by sea from and to the United States. This was the case both during and after the Second World War. This appendix gives an example of one batch of aircraft (F84E Thunderjets from 406 Fighter-Bomber Wing) which passed through Renfrew on their way back to the USA in 1953/1954. The Renfrew arrival dates are approximate and the aircraft arrived from Manston except for ★ from Burtonwood and ★★ from Chateauroux:

Serial Renfrew	Arrival to Mobile	Date of assignment AMA/Sailing date AFB	Arrival Brookley Alabama
49-2023	23 Sep '53★	25 Nov '53	10 Dec '53
49-2032	28 Sep '53★★	2 Feb '54	18 Feb '54
49-2038	22 June '53★	24 June '53	6 July '53
49-2042	Aug '53★★	25 Nov '53	10 Dec '53
49-2045	28 Sep 53★★	25 Nov '53	10 Dec '53
49-2047	10 Nov '53	25 Nov '53	10 Dec '53
49-2051	10 Nov '53	25 Nov '53	10 Dec '53
49-2054	20 Nov '53	2 Feb '54	18 Feb '54
49-2056	10 Nov '53	2 Feb '54	18 Feb '54
49-2059	22 June '53★	24 June '53	6 July '53
49-2060	28 Sep '53★★	25 Nov '53	10 Dec '53
49-2061	4 Nov '53	25 Nov '53	10 Dec '53
49-2063	10 Nov '53	2 Feb '54	18 Feb '54
49-2064	27 June '53	Jan '54	?6 Feb '54
49-2065	10 Nov '53	25 Nov '53	10 Dec '53
49-2066	missing	2 Feb '54	18 Feb '54
49-2068	10 Nov '53	2 Feb '54	18 Feb '54
49-2069	10 Nov '53	25 Nov '53	10 Dec '53
49-2072	4 Nov '53	2 Feb '54	18 Feb '54
49-2073	15 Sep '53★	25 Nov '53	10 Dec '53
49-2075	10 Nov '53	25 Nov '53	10 Dec '53
49-2076	14 Dec '53★	2 Feb '54	18 Feb '54
49-2078	22 Jun '53★	24 June '53	6 July '53
49-2081	4 Nov '53	25 Nov '53	10 Dec '53
49-2082	10 Nov '53	2 Feb '54	18 Feb '54
49-2084	10 Nov '53	2 Feb '54	18 Feb '54
49-2090	4 Nov '53	25 Nov '53	10 Dec '53
49-2094	missing★	25 Nov '53	10 Dec '53

49-2095	4 Nov '53	25 Nov '53	10 Dec '53
49-2097	23 Sep '53★	25 Nov '53	10 Dec '53
49-2099	4 Nov '53	25 Nov '53	10 Dec '53
49-2101	3 Jan '54★★	2 Feb '54	18 Feb '54
49-2102	10 Nov '53	2 Feb '54	18 Feb '54
49-2103	10 Nov '53	25 Nov '53	10 Dec '53
49-2109	9 Nov '53★	2 Feb '54	18 Feb '54
49-2112	5 Nov '53	25 Nov '53	10 Dec '53
49-2117	10 Nov '53	25 Nov '53	10 Dec '53
49-2118	22 June '53	28 Sep '53	?2 Nov '53
49-2121	5 Nov '53	25 Nov '53	10 Dec '53

Details courtesy of Dave Wilton

Bibliography and Sources

Air Pictorial

BAA Annual Report and Accounts 1975–2008

British Airways Archive and Museum, Viscount Way, Building 387 (E121), Heathrow Airport, Hounslow, Middlesex, TW6 2JA

Dugald Cameron, *Glasgow's Airport* (McDougal Publishing)

Dugald Cameron, *A Sense of Place* (Squadron Prints)

Dumbarton Library, Strathleven Place, Dumbarton, G82 1BD – Local History Section contains information relating to Blackburn's operations at Dumbarton.

Fleet Air Arm Museum, RNAS Yeovilton, Near Ilchester, Somerset, BA22 8HT

Flight International

Guy Halford-MacLeod, *Britain's Airlines Volume Two 1951–1964* (The History Press)

Malcolm Fife, *Scottish Aerodromes of the First World War* (The History Press)

Mitchell Library, North Street, Glasgow, G3 7DN – A vast repository of information including, amongst other items, the *Wilf White Collection* of photographs and the movements logs for Renfrew.

Phil Butler, *Liverpool Airport* (The History Press)

Phil Lo Bao, *An Illustrated History of British European Airways* (Browcom)

RAF Millom Aviation and Military Museum, 2 Devonshire Road Industrial Estate, Devonshire Road, Millom, Cumbria, LA18 4JP

RAF Museum (Hendon), Graeme Park Way, London, NW9 5LL

Viking Crash Resource – A group researching the crash of BEA Viking G-AIVE run by James Towill (viking1948@tiscali.co.uk) and Dougie Martindale (dougieandandrea@hotmail.co.uk)

Paisley Central Library, 68 High Street, Paisley, PA1 2BB – Particularly well worth looking at are the old copies of the *Paisley and Renfrewshire Gazette*, held in volumes.

Scottish Flying Club – the name of the defunct SFC has been revived by Colin MacKinnon for the partnership that bought Strathaven Airfield in 2006 from the RAF Benevolent Fund. The original SFC donated Strathaven Airfield, which it founded around 1960, to the RAF Benevolent Fund in the mid-1970s when it was decided to wind up the club. Colin is a good source of information on the activities of the original SFC. Details of the flying operations and flight training of the new Scottish Flying Club can be found on the airfield's website www. strathavenairfield.co.uk.

Internet websites and forums

BAA Glasgow – www.glasgowairport.com (official airport website)
Scotavnet – www.scotavnet.com
Taxiway Alpha – www.taxiwayalpha.com
Airliner World – www.airlinerworld.com
PPRUNE – www.pprune.org.uk
Glasgow Airport – www.egpf.vze.com
Fred Seggie Photographs – www.saap.co.uk

Every effort has been made to check the source of written and photographic material in this book and to gain copyright permission for its use. If a reader finds something they do not agree is correctly referenced could they please contact me through the publisher.

Index

If you are interested in purchasing other books published by The History Press,
or in case you have difficulty finding any History Press books in your local bookshop,
you can also place orders directly through our website
www.thehistorypress.co.uk